THE LIBRARY OF
CONTEMPORARY THOUGHT

*America's most original voices
tackle today's most provocative issues*

JONATHAN KELLERMAN

SAVAGE SPAWN

Reflections on Violent Children

"The most effective way to fight violent crime in the short term is to focus upon habitually violent people when they are very young and not to get distracted by social theorizing that leads nowhere.

"Unfortunately, once again our tendency to empathize gets in the way. After Mitchell Johnson and Andrew Golden were apprehended, Mike Huckabee, the governor of Arkansas, said, 'It makes me angry not so much at individual children that have done it as much as angry at a world in which such a thing can happen.'

"Kindhearted sentiment. Perhaps sincere, or maybe just an attempt by the gov to come across ⋯ ⋯ rm and fuzzy.

"Either way, inane⋯

"The *world* didı⋯ ⋯dren and teachers; two ⋯ ⋯ pay closer attention to the⋯ ⋯em in order to learn what created ⋯ ⋯ow to handle them."

BOOKS BY JONATHAN KELLERMAN

FICTION

ALEX DELAWARE NOVELS

Gone
Rage
Therapy
A Cold Heart
The Murder Book
Flesh and Blood
Dr. Death
Monster
Survival of the Fittest
The Clinic
The Web
Self-Defense
Bad Love
Devil's Waltz
Private Eyes
Time Bomb
Silent Partner
Over the Edge
Blood Test
When the Bough Breaks

OTHER NOVELS

Twisted
Double Homicide (with Faye Kellerman)
The Conspiracy Club
Billy Straight
The Butcher's Theater

NONFICTION

Savage Spawn: Reflections on Violent Children
Helping the Fearful Child
Psychological Aspects of Childhood Cancer

FOR CHILDREN, WRITTEN AND ILLUSTRATED

Jonathan Kellerman's ABC of Weird Creatures
Daddy, Daddy, Can You Touch the Sky?

SAVAGE SPAWN

Reflections on Violent Children

JONATHAN KELLERMAN

THE LIBRARY OF CONTEMPORARY THOUGHT
THE RANDOM HOUSE PUBLISHING GROUP • NEW YORK

The Library of Contemporary Thought
Published by The Random House Publishing Group

Copyright © 1999 by Jonathan Kellerman

Published in the United States by Ballantine Books, an imprint of
The Random House Publishing Group, a division of Random
House, Inc., New York, and simultaneously in Canada by
Random House of Canada Limited, Toronto.

Library of Contemporary Thought and Ballantine and colophon
are registered trademarks and the Library of Contemporary Thought
colophon is a trademark of Random House, Inc.

www.ballantinebooks.com

LIBRARY OF CONGRESS CATALOGING-IN-PUBLICATION DATA
Kellerman, Jonathan.
    Savage spawn : reflections on violent children / Jonathan
Kellerman. — 1st ed.
        p.   cm. — (The library of contemporary thought)
    ISBN 0-345-42939-7 (tr : alk. paper)
    1. Violence in children—United States.   2. Children and violence—
United States.   3. Child psychopathology—United States.
4. Conduct disorders in children—United States.   I. Title.   II. Series:
Library of contemporary thought (Ballantine Publishing Group)
RJ506.V56K45   1999
616.85'82'00835—dc21   98-47234
                                                                    CIP

Text design by Holly Johnson

Cover design by Ruth Ross
Cover photo © Roy McMahon/The Stock Market

Manufactured in the United States of America

First Edition: May 1999

6 8 9 7

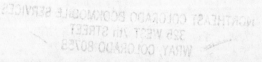

To my young patients, who taught me
so much about the resilience of
the human spirit

I

An Idea That Wouldn't
Go Away

Ⅰ KNOW THE EXACT DAY I decided to write this book.
I love writing novels, am obsessive about writing novels, resent anything that gets in the way of writing
novels. Sometimes this single-mindedness conflicts with
a cranky, highly opinionated disposition, most evident
during the early morning hours, that presses me to
vent spleen in print. Fortunately, a combination of
deep breathing, strong coffee, and solitude usually pre-
vails, and yet another page is added to the mountain of
unwritten letters to the editor and op-ed pieces molder-
ing in some dark corner at the back of my skull.

Thursday, March 26, 1998, was different. My novel
in progress was nearly completed, but I wanted nothing to do with it.

The day before, Mitchell Johnson and Andrew

Golden of Jonesboro, Arkansas, had dressed in camouflage garb, stolen a van, filled it with a tent, a sleeping bag, tools, food, and enormous quantities of ammunition and stolen weapons. Thus equipped, they drove to nearby Westside Middle School, where they set off the fire alarm. As the bells clanged, Johnson and Golden ran for cover behind a wooden ridge, waited for students and teachers to emerge, then unleashed a fusillade. Four little girls and a teacher were killed. Ten other children and a teacher were wounded. A motive was suggested: Mitchell Johnson had been jilted by a girl. No rationale was offered for Andrew Golden's behavior. Both Johnson and Golden had warned other children they were going to kill someone. Both had troubled pasts, but no one took them seriously.

One hundred thirty-four spent shells were found at the crime scene, ranging from rat shot to .357 Magnum bullets. In Andrew Golden's pockets were 312 more shells. Johnson and Golden's arsenal consisted of a .30-06 Remington rifle, a Ruger .44 Magnum rifle, a Universal .30 carbine, a Davis Industry .38 special two-shot, an FIE .380 handgun, a Ruger Security Six .357 revolver, a Remington model 742 .30-06 rifle, a Smith & Wesson .38 pistol, a Double Deuce Buddie two-shot derringer, a Charter Arms .38 special pistol, a Star .380 semiautomatic, six knives, and two speed loaders.

At the time of the attack, Mitchell Johnson was thirteen years old, Andrew Golden eleven.

The Jonesboro massacre wasn't the first of its type—

several other school slaughters carried out by youths had occurred within recent months. Nor would it be the last. Two months later to the day, fifteen-year-old Kipland Kinkel, of Springfield, Oregon, would slay his parents in the family home, steal the family car, drive to Thurston High School, enter the cafeteria, and spray the room with bullets from a semiautomatic rifle, killing two students and wounding twenty-two others. Inadequately searched by the police, Kinkel would be taken into custody with a knife strapped to his leg and, soon after, would attempt to escape by stabbing a cop.

Childhood violence is by no means confined to the bloody rampages of small-town white boys. Drive-by shootings committed by urban gangbangers, usually members of racial and ethnic minorities, proceed with regularity, never attracting the level of media attention and pontification elicited by the Johnsons, Goldens, and Kinkels of our time. A bit of covert racism, perhaps? We don't *expect* it of white kids?

Nevertheless, something about the horror perpetrated by Mitchell Johnson and Andrew Golden seemed especially nauseating: to be so young and yet kill with such a finely honed sense of premeditation.

To be so *cold*.

I'd been trained as a child clinical psychologist, worked for two decades at a major urban hospital and as a private practitioner, had witnessed plenty of psychopathology firsthand. But on March 26, 1998, my education and experience seemed pathetically inadequate.

I struggled to make sense of the rampage. Was there anything I'd learned about human development that could come close to explaining calculated slaughter carried out by a fresh-faced pair who hadn't even nudged puberty?

Mitchell Johnson and Drew Golden's bloody adventure kept me up all night. On Thursday morning I was feeling pretty ragged and no more enlightened. I retired to my office, closed the door, turned off the phone, did a lot of thinking, reviewed dozens of books and scores of scholarly articles, meandered mentally through hundreds of case histories, and thought some more. Then I sat down, composed an essay, and sent it to Glen Nishimura, op-ed editor at *USA Today*, where it was published the following morning.

Late in the afternoon of the twenty-sixth, before I heard back from Nishimura, I received a phone call from my literary agent, Barney Karpfinger. Well aware of my reluctance to interrupt my fiction writing, he wondered nonetheless if I'd consider a nonfiction project: Peter Gethers, vice president and editor at large at Random House, had created a series titled The Library of Contemporary Thought, a collection of short books, issued monthly, authored by established writers on topics that resonated for them personally. My name had come up: Would I be willing to contribute a volume on childhood violence?

"Barney," I said, "I've already started."

II
Tim

THIS KID SCARED ME.

Call him Tim. I've forgotten his name, but Tim will do fine.

He was thirteen but could have passed easily for sixteen. Tall, angular, muscular, tan, with clean-cut good looks, he wore pressed, conservative clothing uninfluenced by the trends of the day, possessed a ready smile, the gift of gab—and a stack of personalized business cards, one of which he handed me as he sat down across from my therapist's chair.

It was the late seventies, a smog-choked California summer, early in the evening. I was working days at Children's Hospital of Los Angeles, conducting research on the psychological effects of catastrophic illness and isolation upon children, setting up psychosocial support systems for kids with cancer and their families, and learning more about human misery and resilience than I'd ever imagined possible.

Nights, I treated private patients, working out of a sublet office in a working-class San Fernando Valley neighborhood, a district of white faces, smallish stucco homes, stingy backyards, pampered pickups, loud motorcycles.

Tim's parents had died in an auto accident when he was eighteen months old and he'd been raised by his grandmother, a well-meaning but noticeably anxious woman in her sixties who projected an air of profound ineptitude. She wasn't happy about seeing a psychologist. In the late seventies, few people outside of Beverly Hills and upper Manhattan were—certainly not the tradesmen and housewives who comprised the bulk of the population in my district. Most of the parents referred to me never called. I didn't mind. It meant that the children who did arrive at my office were more likely to have *real* problems. After all, I was a medical school professor, had no desire to be a high-priced baby-sitter.

Tim's pediatrician had convinced Grandma to bring Tim for evaluation, having exhausted all the advice at his disposal. He termed Grandma "nice but antsy," hoped "some of your behavior modification will help her."

I asked him about any physical ailments Tim might have. He said Tim was one of the healthiest boys he'd ever encountered.

On the face, Tim's presenting problem seemed no different from that of many boys I saw that summer or in summers past: noncompliant behavior and poor school grades. Neither Grandma nor his school could garner much cooperation from him.

As was my custom, first I met with Grandma alone for a history-taking session. Her initial descriptions of Tim's behavior set off no warning signals. The boy didn't "mind," was lax about cleaning his room. Bright and a quick learner, he refused to do homework, was performing below capability, wasn't affected by her attempts at discipline—scolding, yelling, withdrawal of privileges, occasional grounding.

I asked if she thought losing his parents had made an impact upon Tim. Tears welled up in her eyes. Tim's father had been her son, and memories of her own loss, more than a decade past, caused her face to collapse.

No, she finally said. Tim had been too young. He had no recollection of the accident and rarely asked about his parents—she couldn't recall the last time.

I asked if there was anything else she wanted to tell me.

She shook her head, dabbed at her eyes, stared at me full-face. Then something new came into her weary brown irises. Not the usual frustration, anger, fatigue— parental emotions with which I was well acquainted, though I had no children of my own yet.

This was something else, something more than anxiety . . . fear?

She broke the stare, averted her eyes.

"Tim's upsetting you," I said.

"Yes," she said. "Oh, yes."

I waited. Allowed one of those therapeutic silences to hang there for a while. Knowing when to keep the therapeutic mouth shut is as important as—maybe more important than—having something to say.

But these empty seconds evoked nothing. She looked down at her purse. If whatever I'd seen in her eyes remained, the angle of her glance prevented me from confirming it.

Finally she said, "What can you do for me, Dr. Kellerman?"

This early in the game, I had nothing to offer, but I knew she needed to go home with something, so I slung placebo: talked soothingly about gaining Tim's trust, helping Tim focus on what was bothering him, then working together with the two of them to develop a structured behavioral plan. The word *structure* can be reassuring for parents reeling from loss of control. It seemed to offer Grandma a bit of comfort, and she left the office thanking me. But then I saw her eyes again. . . .

A few days later I met Tim. Though I knew I needed to maintain an open mind, I'd come prepared with a suitcaseful of preconceptions.

The game plan I'd outlined for Grandma had been a bit of salesmanship, but I was willing to bet it would turn out to be on target. I'd treated or consulted on hundreds of cases involving noncompliant, under-achieving boys and seemed to work well with that kind of patient, perhaps because I'd been far from compliant during my youth.

The way I saw it, this boy had experienced severe loss and disruption of parental attachment, only to be handed over to a grieving, older woman ill prepared to be a parent again and ambivalent about resuming motherhood. The core problem seemed clear: Grandma had been unable, or unwilling, to set firm limits, and Tim had learned to take advantage of her laxness. What he needed, most likely, was a combination of support and discipline. First thing on the agenda, though, was rapport. Without building a sense of trust, nothing could be accomplished.

Grandma brought him right on time. But she hung near the door and, with that same edginess in her eyes, muttered something about errands to run and quickly exited.

I introduced myself. Tim grinned, stuck out his hand, and pumped mine heartily. That gave me pause. Most kids are apprehensive about visiting any new doctor, let alone a psychologist, but this young man seemed perfectly at home in my waiting room. Grandma had denied any previous psychotherapy. Had she left something out?

I escorted him into the consulting room. He sat

right down opposite me, crossed his legs, stretched, grinned again, said, "Nice place," with all the casualness of a drinking buddy.

The grin hung there, big and wide and . . . Was I overinterpreting when I sensed a mocking quality?

I asked him if this was the first time he'd ever seen a psychologist.

"Yup." Still grinning. Not a trace of nervousness.

With a flourish, he whipped out a stack of glossy black business cards and handed me one. His name was printed in the center, in oversized silver script, above a phone number.

"Nice card," I said.

"Got to have one if you're in business."

"What business are you in?"

His smile stretched. He started to yawn, covered it. Chuckled. Said, "Anything to make money."

"Been doing okay making money?"

"Great. How about you?" he said.

"Fine, thanks."

"Bet you make a lot of money."

"Making money's important to you?"

"Hey," he said, "with money you can buy anything."

"What kinds of things do you do to make money?"

"Stuff," he said. "Favors."

"Favors?"

"Like if someone needs some help with something, I help 'em."

"What kind of help?"

He stretched like a young lion. "If someone's bugging someone and they want it to stop, I make it stop."

"You make it stop," I said. "And you get paid for it."

He pointed a finger gun in my direction. "Correct."

"Kind of like a bodyguard."

He laughed. "Guess so."

"Got any other businesses?"

"Sure. I sell stuff."

"Stuff?"

"Magazines, candy. Sold a bike last week."

"A bike?" I said.

"Found it on the street." The grin stretched.

"Someone just left a bike on the street."

"Must've been someone stupid." Laughter. "I don't sell everything. Some stuff I give away."

"What kind of stuff?"

"To girls. I get them stuff and give it to them free." He recrossed his legs, sat back, let one hand rest on a thigh.

Then he winked.

"The girls get stuff free," I said.

He laughed again. "They give me stuff back. In trade." He licked his lips. Reached into his pocket, pulled out a pack of cigarettes and a chrome-plated lighter. "Okay if I smoke?"

"Sorry, no."

Shrugging, he put the pack back but kept the lighter out, passing it from hand to hand.

"Been smoking long?"

Shrug. No more smile. Being refused had changed his demeanor. Now his long, handsome face was immobile, placid.

More than calm. Emotionless.

Dead-eyed.

He yawned again. Looked at his watch. Expensive watch for a thirteen-year-old.

"Do you know why you're here, Tim?"

Shrug.

"Your grandmother's been having some problems with you."

Shrug.

"She feels she can't get you to obey her."

"She's stupid."

"Stupid?"

He laughed. "She's a stupid asshole. Doesn't know what's flying. She's old." He turned the last two words into the lowest epithet. But still no anger; the lack of passion made the little speech more vicious.

"Has she been mean to you?"

The question amused him. He shook his head. "She's just a stupid asshole."

"She's been raising you since you were a baby."

"Yup."

He began looking around the office. I used the time to contemplate my next move. Was it the right time to raise the topic of his parents' death, or should I wait? Normally I'd have held back, but the complete lack of tension in Tim's speech and posture intrigued me. At that point I was unwilling to believe anyone so young could be so dispassionate, so nakedly cruel.

Defensiveness; had to be. This kid was so armored he had to hide behind a macho facade.

Would broaching the subject cause the armor to crack too suddenly?

On the other hand, not raising it could be a serious mistake. Most teens had their BS detectors set to high. Tim fancied himself streetwise, cool, and collected, and he seemed reasonably bright. He might interpret avoidance of the obvious as evidence I wasn't being straight.

His eyes were back on mine now. Blue, still. The grin had also returned.

Definitely smug.

I said, "Your grandmother raised you because your parents passed away."

"Yeah!" he exclaimed, as if I were a quiz show contestant who'd guessed right.

That threw me. Were his defenses so calcified that he'd moved a universe beyond hurt?

I said, "What do you remember about your parents?"

"My dad was a pilot." He pantomimed a swooping jet. "Cool guy."

"And your mom?"

He shot to his feet, as if on cue. "Want to see a picture?"

Ah, he carries a snapshot. So he does care.

"Sure."

Out came an expensive-looking leather billfold from which he withdrew a small, creased photo that he handed to me.

A good-looking couple in their twenties stood hand in hand against a backdrop of greenery.

"That's her," said Tim, pointing to the woman. Smirking. "Major piece of ass, huh?"

I HAD ONE MORE SESSION with Tim during which he boasted of having had sex with over a dozen girls. In several cases he claimed to have collected their panties, which he sold to other boys. He produced a packet of condoms as evidence. He also crowed about trafficking in a variety of other "found" goods but would offer no further details. He denied using drugs but winked when I asked if he ever sold dope.

All of this was delivered in an even, strangely un-modulated voice that nevertheless managed to brim with self-satisfaction. His braggadocio assumed a pruri-ence that clogged the room. I steered the conversation to his schoolwork. He dismissed me with a wave of his hand. Improving his grades was out of the question because school was stupid and wouldn't help him attain his goal of being a "big businessman." No, he owed nothing to his grandmother for taking him in. It had been her decision, he still thought she was a stupid asshole.

He never displayed a whit of anxiety, rarely blinked.

I realized I'd been wrong. There was no wall of defenses. He had nothing against which to defend because he was truly untroubled.

Completely different from the other noncompliant boys I'd seen.

It was as if I were sitting across from a member of another species.

Toward the end of the second session I did witness a single flare of strong emotion. He asked again if he could smoke, and when I turned him down, his eyes narrowed to slits. Then he favored me with another kind of smile—knowing, focused. Hateful. His body remained loose, at ease, his voice flat, but the anger coalesced in his eyes. He spread his legs. Touched his inner thigh briefly. Winked.

Occupying the office as if he owned it.

I reminded myself he was only thirteen.

When he left, I made sure he exited first. He knew I was watching his back. Stopping at the door to the waiting room, he made a sudden move with his shoulder, as if about to butt me. I recoiled. He checked the movement, a classic bullying technique. *Faked you out!*

Then he turned to me. Winked again.

Before I could say anything, Grandma was opening

the door. I asked to talk to her, but she said she had to rush somewhere.

Tim chuckled and saluted. "Bye, Doc."

He swaggered down the hall ahead of her. Pulled out his cigarettes. She said something to him. All I could make out was a whining tone. He lit up and increased the distance between them.

T HAT NIGHT I PHONED HER at home. She was out, didn't return the call or the three others that followed. Two days before the next appointment, she reached my answering service and canceled, citing a time conflict. I called her again. No answer. She never rescheduled.

I reached Tim's pediatrician, filled him in, venturing that Tim might very well be a budding psychopath.

"Really?" he said. "Yeah, I can see that. He *was* kind of slick."

"You might want to talk to his grandmother about it."

"Think so? And tell her what?"

"At the very least, to be careful."

"That sounds scary, Jon."

"He's a scary kid."

A few weeks later he'd received a message of his

own from Grandma. She and Tim had moved to another city, where she planned to put him in military school.

Over the next few years I scanned the papers for mention of the boy with the glossy black business cards, wondering if he'd show up in the crime blotter, or perhaps—and this was my therapeutic optimism at work—on some roster of heroic soldiering.

As time went on, I encountered a few—mercifully few—other boys like him. All displayed the same emotional flatness, lack of conscience, grating bravado, inflated self-esteem, ambitious pleasure seeking. All disparaged those who loved them. All had engaged in criminal behavior. Some had already been incarcerated.

None cared to change. None changed.

I don't know what happened to Tim, but I have plenty of fantasies on the subject.

Maybe he was smart enough to avoid a life of crime. Perhaps he even buckled down sufficiently to become an entrepreneur whose worst offenses involved no bloodletting. Maybe he went into politics as a behind-the-scenes manipulator.

Probably not, though. He had no appetite for any kind of work.

Most probably he's done terrible things.

III

A Species Apart

THERE ARE TWO IMPORTANT REASONS for taking a hard look at antisocial children.

First, youthful offenders pose a serious social problem by themselves. There is strong evidence that although the level of violent crime may be dropping in some parts of the United States, it continues to rise among the young. As a recent epidemiologic study stated, "Adolescents are now experiencing the highest and most rapidly increasing rates of lethal and nonlethal violence. The increase in violence among youths 10 to 14 years of age is especially important and alarming"(1).

Second, and perhaps more important, are the disquieting findings that antisocial behavior in childhood often lays the foundations for a durable pattern of adult criminality and that the older the child is at the time we reach him, the less likely we are to be able to modify his behavior (2). If kids like Tim changed their ways miraculously upon completing puberty, we would have little interest in them. It is the matriculation to chronic criminality—the natural history of habitual evil—that concerns us.

Unfortunately, when it comes to crime, the child is, indeed, father to the man: the most seriously antisocial children share a constellation of personality traits with the most seriously adult criminals—psychopathy (3–6). In order to appreciate fully the magnitude of childhood criminality as a social destructor, it is best to begin at the endpoint—the terrible people that violent, antisocial kids are likely to become.

This is not to say that all children with violent tendencies are psychopaths. But young psychopaths comprise a substantial proportion of the children who devolve into serious, habitual criminals. And what criminals they become! The cruelest, most calculating felons. Blithe killers, strong-arm virtuosos, industrious career miscreants viewing crime as their profession, unfettered by conscience or convention or the threat of distant punishment as they wreak misery and pain on the rest of us. They're not spurred by poverty or rage against one machine or another, though these factors may play a role in their development.

They do it because they *love* it.

They do it because they *can*.

Prison keeps them away from the rest of us, but once they get out of prison, their recidivism rate is significantly higher than that of other released convicts (7). They don't stop being bad because they don't *want* to stop being bad. If they live past the age of fifty, their criminal behavior tends to taper off, but more for lack of energy than because of any moral repair. They are capable of dishing out some nasty surprises at any age.

What turns them on is the kick, the high, the slaking of impulse—pure sensation. Power, dominance, subjugation of the rest of us.

The *fun* of crime.

They commit the outrages that we mislabel as "senseless crimes." We're wrong about that, just as we are about most of the assumptions we make about psychopathic criminals. Because we view their behavior through the lens of our normalcy, apply *our* moral logic to *their* amoral world.

Their crimes make *perfect* sense to them.

Not all gang members are psychopaths. Some are just stupid kids drifting along with a bad crowd, adolescent conformists in lockstep with mean-streets norms, cowards seeking the shelter of group protection, or lonely, neglected, abused kids craving the structure of a surrogate family.

But gang *leaders* almost always *are* psychopaths.

Psychopaths may not always pull the trigger—though they have no compunction about doing so. Sometimes it's simply more convenient to get an underling to do the job. But inevitably they're the architects of the drive-bys and the holdups, the devisers and contractors of drug scams, con games, protection rackets, killings for hire.

At the peak of their game, if they're relatively intelligent, they can attain major positions of leadership—cartel kings, Mafia dons, violent cult leaders, genocidal dictators.

Think of a cocktail party with Ted Bundy and Vlad the Impaler at the top of the guest list. And, hey, there's Al Capone sharing trade secrets with Pol Pot, Carlos the Jackal bending elbows with Jack the Ripper and Pablo Escobar, Jeffrey Dahmer and John Gacy discussing art. Wow, look at all those politicians and studio heads, and good old Charles Keating with his Cheshire grin, unperturbed by all those old people plunged into financial ruin. All of them sharing an unbridled lust for power, control, and sensation, as well as a blithe lack of regard for the feelings of others.

Of course, that would be a psychopathic A-list. The very smartest psychopaths from the most privileged backgrounds often avoid violence, because they know it's likely to get them into trouble and they have safer means of exploitation at their disposal. Garden-variety psychopaths, lacking the brains, luck, will, and attention span for criminal celebrity or legitimate enterprise, comprise a high proportion of the criminal bourgeoisie, going about their business like any other bunch of working stiffs.

Conning, robbing, stealing, killing, getting busted, going to jail, getting out, conning, robbing, stealing, killing, getting busted . . .

Psychopathic tendencies begin very early in life—as young as three—and they endure. The same goes for pathological aggressiveness. One study of coldly, cruelly aggressive children produced clear evidence of violence beginning around the age of six and a half (8). Several reviews of childhood murderers revealed strong patterns of prehomicidal violence by early adolescence, with some kids manifesting frightening tendencies as young as two (9–13).

Violent sexuality and psychopathy don't always go together, but when violent sexual imagery is tossed into the psychic mulch that twists the roots of an antisocial youngster, the strangler vine that pokes through often sprouts into a monstrosity well beyond the blackest nightmares created by Dr. Moreau.

Sexual psychopaths learn to manipulate and victimize early, sniffing out vulnerability and weakness with the acuity of heat-seeking missiles. They begin with victims who can't complain—animals, and hone their skills tormenting, killing, and mutilating, before moving on to human prey (14).

They're the bullies, the stalkers, the malicious sneaks, smooth victimizers like Bundy, able to morph from disarmingly charming conversationalists into purveyors of violence so suddenly that it stuns and incapacitates their victims well before the horror of what's really happening sinks in.

We're rarely, if ever, prepared for them, because their capacity for cruelty stretches far beyond the limits imposed on our imagination by civilization. We don't *think* as they do.

When confronted by spectacularly grotesque expressions of psychopathy, we engage in armchair psychiatry, mouthing seemingly logical platitudes such as "They're crazy. You'd have to be crazy to cut off someone's head and freeze it, or mutilate a ten-year-old, or shoot up a schoolyard."

Defense attorneys capitalize on this.

But it's a lie. You don't have to be crazy.

Psychopathic killers are anything *but* crazy.

Insanity, a legal term rather than a medical diagnosis, varies in definition from state to state. But all concepts of insanity have in common the notion that the insane criminal suffers from a biologically mediated inability to distinguish right from wrong and/or an inability to assist in his own defense.

Psychopaths know exactly what they're doing.

Sometimes their motive is nothing more than the alleviation of boredom.

They get bored easily.

Sometimes a psychopathic child's cruelty tops off at the level of schoolyard bullying. But often it doesn't, because domination, like any other narcotic, breeds satiation and habituation. When first shoving, then hurting, and then raping cease to provide a sufficiently potent thrill, the game can swell, peaking at the ultimate control scheme.

That's when psychopaths try out murder. If they

like the taste of it, get away with it, they try to relive the thrill of domination using memory, but that rarely works because they're not good at coaxing forth mental imagery. So they tend to collect souvenirs, anything from trinkets to body parts. And when those mementos no longer work, the obvious solution is to do it again. And again.

When impoverished imagination limits them to repetition, we end up with that cliché of bad TV: the serial killer.

Psychopaths are the villains who perpetrate a certain *type* of serial killing—what the FBI with its penchant for classification calls "organized."

The other side of the coin is the disorganized serial killer, who *is* crazy: a malnourished, low-IQ madman tormented by delusions (distorted thoughts) that drive him to murder: *Mrs. Jones next door is the Antichrist, and for the last three months she's been sneaking into my room and implanting electrodes that hiss "666" into my brain.*

Disorganized serial killers run amok without warning, often slaughtering wildly, making little or no effort to conceal their crimes or to clean up the evidence, simplifying the policeman's lot: just look for the filthy ectomorph in bloody clothes lurching down Main Street muttering to himself.

Organized serial murderers are quite another bunch: crafty, meticulous planners of death, they often come across as attractive and personable. Conventional-looking, they are often involved in outwardly stable relationships, though they are only faking intimacy. Not as smart as they think they are, but bright enough to have decent job skills, they may accumulate the trappings of a normal life, with steady work and a decent income—often augmented by crime. They like their quiet time, though. Enjoy driving empty roads. The thrill for them is as much in the planning as the outcome. Frequently sadistic, they are utterly remorseless.

Anyone who stalks, rapes, murders, decapitates, and disembowels without feeling must be crazy, right?

Wrong.

No hallucinations clutter their heads. *Any* sort of mental picture comes hard for them.

Psychopaths sleep well at night. Unusually soundly (15).

If they're caught, they often try to *fake* madness, because crime evokes punishment while illness draws forth sympathy. Back in the sixties and seventies it worked quite often. Nowadays jurors are more skeptical, so it seldom does. Psychopaths aren't as clever as they think they are.

At least the ones who get caught aren't. Then again, jailed psychopaths are failed psychopaths, so all of our data on criminals may be drawn from a biased sample of incompetents. The best and the brightest serial slayers might be racking up triple-digit victim tallies no one even knows about.

That's part of what creates a problem for the FBI's much-vaunted psychological profiles of psychopathic killers.

Profiles are based upon information gleaned from crime scenes and interviews with *imprisoned* psychopathic killers. But what about crime scenes that are never discovered? Killers who live out their lives undetected? And psychopaths are expert liars, so even the data they feed inquisitive special agents need to be regarded with a good deal of skepticism.

That's why certain of today's "facts" derived from psychological profiles degrade into tomorrow's revealed misconception.

Such as the "rule" that serial killers never murder outside their race. Till they do. Or that women are never serial killers. Till they are.

Profiles are most effective as career builders for retired FBI agents seeking to be best-selling authors and consultants to the film industry, but they miss the mark as often as they hit. Profiling rarely, if ever, catches killers in big cities, though in smaller communities it may help direct the police toward a suspect pool.

When organized psychopaths are apprehended, it's almost always due to plodding police work, a mistake by the bad guy, or a combination of the two. Once the authorities have a killer in tow, the profile may be examined. If the facts fit the prophecy, a press conference is held. If not, no one talks about it.

It's not the FBI's fault. They're doing the best they

can with the skimpy knowledge stored in their hard drives. No one really understands psychopathy.

Biological theories of antisocial behavior abound, but no medication has been found that alters antisocial behavior. Conventional psychotherapy is useless, because therapy depends upon insight and a desire to change, and psychopaths possess neither. For the same reason, penal rehabilitation of habitual criminals based upon teaching job skills is a dismal failure and will continue to be so.

Applying the concept of voluntary social change to well-developed psychopaths has all the value of sweeping the ocean with a whisk broom to prevent pollution.

Rehabilitation, like most of our mistakes in dealing with psychopaths, stems from our viewing them through the lens of our own psyches and experiences, as we empathize, analyze, search for common ground, assume humanity where none exists.

They're different.

Though they may engage in savagery, they can appear anything but unrefined. Nor does a cold soul imply lack of artistic sensibility. Psychopaths may be creative, talented, even gifted—one has only to view a prison art show or listen to a prison band to appreciate this. But that has nothing to do with their psychopathy. I have written previously about numerous gifted artists who murdered, including bona fide geniuses such as Caravaggio, and others, such as Gauguin, who knowingly infected young girls with syphilis with an aplomb that suggests psychopathic cruelty (16).

Psychiatrist Thomas Millar, in an eloquent essay titled "The Age of Passion Man," written nearly two decades ago, decried the tendency of contemporary Western society to glamorize hedonism and antisocial behavior, and to confuse psychopathy, which he regards as a form of malignant childishness, with heroism (17).

"Some [psychopaths]," Millar writes, "manage to cling to the omnipotent illusions, but the price they pay is the loss of their humanity. A few, like [T. E.] Lawrence and Hitler, manage, for a brief span, to persuade the world to endorse their illusion of power . . . but ultimately the game proves too real, and when the bloody facts can no longer be denied, the mask of omnipotence falls away, and the petulant child stands revealed."

Confusing creativity with morality and psychopathic rebelliousness with social liberation led Norman Mailer to predict that psychopaths would turn out to be the saviors of society (18). Mailer was as terribly wrong about that as he was when he worked hard to spring career criminal Jack Henry Abbott from prison. Shortly after his release, Abbott murdered an innocent man. Oops. What impressed Mailer were Abbott's writings, summarized in a thin book titled *In the Belly of the Beast*. A coolheaded review of this volume nearly two decades later reveals it to be a crude, nasty,

sophomoric collection of self-justifying diatribes—
prototypical psychopathy.

Muddled thinking about evil is by no means limited to the political left. Sex murderer Edgar Herbert
Smith, sentenced to execution for raping and blud-
geoning a fifteen-year-old girl to death with a baseball
bat, was able to turn a phrase with some skill, and he
conned William Buckley into thinking *he* was innocent. Buckley campaigned to get Smith out of prison,
finally succeeding in 1971, whereupon Smith promptly
and viciously attacked another woman. Smith then ad-
mitted that he'd been guilty of the first murder. Oops
again.

During the fifties, sixties, and seventies, overly ro-
mantic notions of psychopathy within the so-called
artistic community led to tremendous sympathy being
directed toward criminals such as Caryl Chessman and
Huey Newton. How sadly off target. Chessman was a
cold-blooded serial rapist, and Newton was a violent
thug and a drug pusher masquerading as a political
reformer.

Perhaps the most horrifying example of good intentions paving the road to hell involved a charming
fellow named Jack Unterwegger, an Austrian career
criminal. After being released from a life sentence in
response to agitation from European literati who judged
his poetry indicative of a soul made whole, Unterwegger quickly resumed his real career: murdering women

at a rapid, relentless pace. Eleven women in Austria, Czechoslovakia, and the United States were abused, raped, and strangled to death with their brassieres. Double oops. Sorry.

That's eleven victims the police *know* about, because if Unterwegger was like other psychopathic criminals, he accomplished many more crimes than the ones for which he was arrested.

A lot more. In addition to unreported crimes, another factor exists to deflate crime rates: plea bargaining, which by compressing several offenses into one criminal charge presents an overly rosy view of the incidence of felonies. This applies even to the most violent offenses. One group of serial rapists studied by the FBI were convicted of an average of seven attacks but in fact committed an average of twenty-eight rapes each (19). And those were only the *known* assaults. The actual number was most likely considerably higher. How much higher? We'll never know. The bad guys aren't telling where the bodies are buried.

(I've been using and will continue to use *he, him,* and *his* because male psychopaths outnumber female psychopaths and because males are responsible for a very high proportion, probably 90 percent or more, of violent crimes.)

The wrongdoings for which career criminals are apprehended, put on trial, and incarcerated represent *a very small proportion of the evil they actually commit.* Add the fact that a small core of repetitive, habitual psychopaths who begin their criminal careers as young children are responsible for an astoundingly large proportion of the misdemeanors and felonies that blight our lives, and it's easy to see why increased reliance upon stupid procedures that keep psychopaths among us, such as plea bargaining, parole, probation, and "alternative sentencing," have helped create an America plagued by nightmarish crime rates.

When smart police officials, such as those in New York, decide to lock up career bad guys no matter what the offense, crime rates plummet. The same goes for "three strikes" laws that incarcerate repeat offenders for life.

When it comes to sentencing, academic distinctions between nonviolent and violent crime are less important than pinpointing the *type* of criminal at the docket. The otherwise law-abiding jerk who commits a one-time assault during a bar brawl is of much less threat to society than is the supposedly nonviolent con man who's been preying on marks for two decades, because you can bet the con man has committed scores of felonies in addition to con games that have never come to light. You can also bet he's unlikely to have much compunction about using violence if it suits his purposes.

During a recent visit to a California state hospital for the criminally insane, I learned that the number of psychopaths trying to fake insanity has mushroomed because the bad guys are running scared from the state's "three strikes" law. Though psychopaths are less affected by fear and punishment than normal people, they do respond to the threat of negative consequences that are *severe and relatively immediate*. Nebulous or long-term risks are likely to have little or no effect upon them because they have a great deal of difficulty, perhaps biologically mediated, in dealing with time and in connecting distant consequences to their behavior (20–22). For that reason, the death penalty as it is carried out in contemporary America, with decades passing between the imposition of sentence and execution, is unlikely to serve as an effective deterrent. However, societies where execution is carried out swiftly, such as Saudi Arabia, have found the death penalty to be extremely effective. The deterrent capabilities of capital punishment are also illustrated historically by social changes that occurred in Elizabethan England when hanging was discontinued as a punishment for a host of crimes, including pickpocketing, due to humanitarian agitation. The almost immediate result was a huge rise in the rate of pickpocketing.

But debates about the death penalty are so emotionally laden that they tend to serve as red herrings, distracting us from preventive solutions. The most effective way to fight violent crime in the short term is to focus upon habitually violent people when they are very young and not to get distracted by social theorizing that leads nowhere.

Unfortunately, once again our tendency to empathize gets in the way. After Mitchell Johnson and Andrew Golden were apprehended, Mike Huckabee, the governor of Arkansas, said, "It makes me angry not so much at individual children that have done it as much as angry at a world in which such a thing can happen" (23).

Kindhearted sentiment. Perhaps sincere, or maybe just an attempt by the gov to come across as warm and fuzzy.

Either way, inane.

The *world* didn't fire 134 bullets at innocent children and teachers; two *individuals* did. And we'd better pay close attention to them and to others like them in order to learn what created them and how to handle them.

Johnson and Golden's tender age led to much discussion about the ultimate disposition of their fates. The notion of an eleven-year-old and a thirteen-year-old locked up for life tugs at our heartstrings, and legions of experts exist who are willing to testify that such boys should not be held responsible for their acts because they are mentally ill, and that because of their youth they can be rehabilitated. But any doctors attempting to promulgate a defense based on diminished mental capacity for the type of calculated, well-planned violence accomplished by Golden and Johnson would be at best in error and at worst perjurers in the service of fat fees and prime-time exposure.

In terms of the possibility of rehabilitation, no one can say for sure, but bear in mind that experts are notoriously poor predictors of future violence and that, given the risks, the most sensible criteria to use when determining the fates of young cold-blooded killers should be facts on the ground: These prepubescent villains have committed crimes so premeditated, vicious, and evil that I feel they should preclude reentry into noncriminal society at any time. Unfortunately, Arkansas law provided only for the incarceration of Johnson and Golden until the age of twenty-one. When those boys get out, watch your back.

Lock up the psychopaths for as long as possible, and the streets will be safer. Keep the psychopaths away from the rest of us as completely as possible, and quality of life will soar.

The sad truth is that there *are* bad people.

Forget all that situational-ethics gibberish about fine distinctions between good and evil, excuses about how we all sin from time to time, how there's really no such thing as abnormal, merely variants along a subtle continuum. True, very few of us are saints. But that has nothing to do with serious crime. Or with psychopaths.

Bad people are really *different*.

IV

The Nature of the Beast

A MAJOR CLARIFICATION: I'M TALKING about *psycho-paths*, not *psychotics*.

These two terms are often erroneously used interchangeably by the popular press as well as by those who should know better, but other than beginning with *psych-* they have virtually nothing in common. In fact, in some sense they are polar opposites.

Psychotics suffer from serious mental disorders of thought and emotion, probably biologically caused. The most common psychoses are the schizophrenias, a group of diseases, sometimes acute but more often chronic, featuring disintegration—*not splitting*—of personality. Schizophrenics represent between 1 and 4 percent of the population in virtually every society studied and suffer from confused and grossly distorted thoughts (delusions) and perceptions (hallucinations), extreme reliance upon internal stimulation (withdrawal and autism), impoverished thinking and language, and, more often than not, extremely high levels of anxiety and/or depression.

Contrary to the nonsensical theories of authors such as British psychiatrist R. D. Laing, who attained prominence during the 1960s with the notion that schizophrenia is glamorous, artistic, and poetic, madmen live in a dark, jumbled world of pain and torment. This is true mental illness.

The claim that schizophrenics are less violent than normal people has been bandied about, but the data indicate otherwise: Madmen do exhibit a higher rate of homicide than the rest of us, most frequently when their delusions direct them to harm someone (24). The worst-case example of schizophrenic violence is the aforementioned disorganized serial killer.

There is also a small subsample of murderous adolescents whose crimes appear to result from psychosis (25). These youngsters exhibit the same symptoms as do adult psychotic murderers—paranoia, command hallucinations (voices telling them to kill), and delusions (distorted thoughts, often about their victims). But the overall incidence of schizophrenic crime, especially child schizophrenic crime, remains low. Furthermore, the felonies of the mad, though often devastating, tend to be impulsive, nonrepetitive, and easily detected. Rusty Weston's 1998 Capitol shooting, resulting in the murder of two guards, was an example of an inadequately treated schizophrenic wreaking tragedy. But schizophrenics do not prey habitually on society, nor do they contribute significantly to our crime rate.

The same is true of those individuals suffering from the other primary psychotic classification, manic-depression—a disorder of affect (mood) in which emotions swing between severe depression and mental hyperactivity. Manic-depression is almost certainly biologically based. In addition to featuring dramatically increased rates of behavior, the manic phase may also involve some behaviors that resemble psychopathy, such as inflated self-esteem and excessive involvement in illogical and quixotic activities.

In her brilliant book *An Unquiet Mind*, noted psychologist and mood researcher Kay Redfield Jamison describes one of her own manic episodes, during which she marched to the pharmacy and purchased dozens of earthquake survival kits. Manic individuals may also get involved in foolish financial schemes, both as perpetrators and as victims, and their mood shifts can be so severe that their grasp of reality is impaired, leading to a variant of what Jamison unsparingly terms "madness" (26).

There is a slightly increased risk of violence among some manic-depressives, particularly during untreated manic phases, but once again, mania does not account for a high proportion of habitual criminality. And manic-depression is one of the mental illnesses for which there is consistently effective treatment.

Most manic-depressives and at least a third of schizophrenics can be managed very well using medication and backup psychotherapy. Another third of schizophrenics respond partially but may continue to require institutionalization. The remaining third are resistant to treatment.

To sum up, psychotics are the people we think of as crazy. Untreated or incompletely treated psychotics may explode one day and do something terrible, but they are generally too disordered to plan, plot, or calculate repetitive felonies and too cognitively fragmented to achieve *any* kind of stable career, including that of habitual crime.

Look to the psychopaths for that kind of thing.

V

Evil as an Affliction?

Psychopathy is something quite different from madness. Classified by psychiatrists and psychologists as *a disorder of character or personality*, psychopathy involves no loss of reason nor any increase in depression, agitation, and anxiety. On the contrary, psychopaths are lucid and free of angst, inner doubt, insecurities, or neurotic torment.

Mitchell Johnson and Andrew Golden were described as unruffled when apprehended. (Later, though, when locked up, they cried for their mothers. The charitable interpretation of this emotional display was that the boys had suddenly gotten in touch with the enormity of the evil they'd caused. A more cynical though perhaps more reasonable spin is simply self-pity.) This remote coolness was also shown by Kipland Kinkel and is common in many killers, young or otherwise. It is also characteristic of psychopathic criminals in general.

How many times have we heard the postoutrage cry of astonishment from neighbors and casual acquaintances: "He was always so quiet. Didn't seem upset at all"? No surprise there. Psychopaths often appear to be preternaturally calm (more on this later).

Psychopathy baffles psychiatrists and psychologists, and as stymied experts so frequently do, they have responded by *relabeling*. And because we're talking about the fractious world of mental health, where pseudoreligious dogma and economic motives often masquerade as science, the labeling process has also been impacted by politics.

Consider the linguistic shift that occurred during the late sixties and early seventies, when psychopathy, with its implication of disease and individual irregularity, proved a poor ideological fit with then-reigning, Marxist-derived social science norms that cast crime as a consequence of economic and social oppression. (Remember "All black men are political prisoners"?)

According to Marxist and neo-Marxist criminological doctrine, society was sick and oppressive, while deviant individuals, even violent offenders, were poets, urban guerrillas, and freedom fighters—Promethean heroes struggling against institutional fascism. Today this malicious apologia is clung to most enthusiastically by the far right: Blow up hundreds of people in the Oklahoma City Federal Building and you're a latter-day Tom Paine. But back in the late sixties and early seventies, social liberalism had its way with the criminal justice system. Prison sentences were radically shortened, the back wards of mental hospitals were unlatched, and efforts were made to integrate career criminals and the severely mentally ill into society, with disastrous results on both fronts. Alcoholism and drug abuse, common in both criminals and psychiatric patients, soared during the seventies, eighties, and early nineties, as did crime rates. Social reformers were baffled by the "sudden" appearance of a "homeless problem."

Societal frustration finally led to outcries for more punishment and less counseling, but some of the old naïveté remains. Recently I heard an "expert" bemoan the fact that so much money was being spent on prisons instead of schools. As if the two were mutually exclusive. As if schooling psychopaths will turn them into model citizens.

The social theorists of the sixties and seventies mugged language as well. "Riots" were upgraded to "insurrections," "terrorists" to "freedom fighters." (This playing fast and loose with the language endures to this day in the world press. It all depends, of course, upon whose ox is being gored. When the PLO blew up school buses in Israel, they were termed guerrillas and freedom fighters by American journalists. The Islamic extremists who blew up American embassies in the Middle East and East Africa were quickly excoriated as terrorists by the same correspondents.)

During the sixties and seventies, psychopaths were refashioned as *sociopaths*. No longer ill, they were now judged to be victims of persecution.

Not that this had any salubrious effect upon rates of robbery, rape, and murder. On the contrary, de-emphasizing personal responsibility allowed for the continuation of social policies, such as alternative sentencing, early release, and mainstreaming of dangerous criminals into our neighborhoods, that boosted crime statistics.

So a decade later, when advances in molecular structure and genetics caused a rush to biologize human behavior, the time was ripe for yet another episode of the Rename Game. This belief that every type of behavior has an underlying, traceable biological cause stemmed from an academically generated and media-fed campaign based on tantalizing but very sketchy data. Because journalists tend to be scientifically unsophisticated and eager for print space, they often serve as gullible conduits for the unsubstantiated claims of supposed sages in white coats.

Science accomplishes wonderful things, but even the hardest science lurches along dim pathways that are shadowed by biases, hunches, and guesswork. Scientists are seldom as knowledgeable—or as effective—as they claim to be.

Decades after the initial hoopla promulgated by the biological determinists, the level of understanding about the causes and mechanisms of mental and behavioral problems remains primitive, even in instances where medical treatments have proved highly effective, such as medication for psychosis and depression. Thus, we are much better at suppressing schizophrenic symptoms with Thorazine than at figuring out why and how Thorazine works.

In psychiatry and psychology, most biological explanations have centered around insufficient or disrupted levels of a neurotransmitter (brain chemical) called serotonin, but irregularities in serotonin have been used to explain every psychiatric symptom from obsessive-compulsive behavior to psychosis to depression to psychopathy, creating what is essentially a neurochemical wastebasket with no power to predict or discriminate between individual disorders.

And once again politics rears its nasty little head. For as the health-care dollar shrinks and jockeying for patients among mental health professionals intensifies, each discipline heads for the heavy artillery. In the case of psychiatrists, it's the medical degree, and organized psychiatry has fought to medicalize as many behavioral deviances as possible in order to attain control over treatment delivery (and reimbursement).

Psychiatric logic is that if it's a disease, only a physician should treat it. This exact argument was used decades earlier, unsuccessfully, when psychiatrists tried to restrict non-M.D.'s from practicing psychotherapy. Today few psychiatrists would claim any primacy in the delivery of the "talking cure," and in fact many psychiatrists denigrate psychotherapy as a lower-level service best relegated to paraprofessionals (under a psychiatrist's supervision, of course).

As part of the campaign to medicalize deviance, the American Psychiatric Association began producing a series of *Diagnostic and Statistical Manuals*, small-print, phone-directory-sized tomes chock-full of numerical diagnostic codes easily adaptable for computerized insurance billing. Known as DSMs—the current model is number IV—these volumes have become the billing bibles of the mental health industry.

I am not dismissing the DSMs as mere political tools. Much of the research they've generated is excellent and has gone a long way toward getting mental health professionals to think scientifically about psychological disorders. *Any* systematic classification is certainly an improvement over the sloppy, often opinion-based diagnostic taxonomy of the past.

The problem is one of overzealous application: Some disorders simply don't lend themselves to the disease model, and nowhere is this truer than in the case of psychopathy/sociopathy, which, whether you view it as a dysfunction of the individual or as a reaction to societal oppression, or even as chemistry gone wrong, persists in sounding a lot more like nasty behavior than an illness.

That, of course, creates tremendous cognitive dissonance among psychiatrists, psychologists, and other mental health workers. It's an economic threat as well. Why pay clinicians of any stripe to treat meanness and viciousness, or acts of protest grounded in the struggle against oppression?

Hence a new syndrome: *antisocial personality disorder* (DSM 301.70), or APD.

Let's examine the DSM description of APD: "A history of continuous and chronic antisocial behavior in which the rights of others are violated, persistence into adult life of a pattern of antisocial behavior that began before the age of 15, and failure to sustain good job performance over a period of several years (although this may not be evident in individuals who are self-employed or who have not been in a position to demonstrate this feature, e.g. students or housewives). The antisocial behavior is not due to either severe Mental Retardation, Schizophrenia, or manic episodes.

"Lying, stealing, fighting, truancy, and resisting authority are typical early childhood signs. In adolescence, unusually early or aggressive sexual behavior, excessive drinking, and use of illicit drugs are frequent. In adulthood, these kinds of behavior continue, with the addition of inability to sustain consistent work performance or to function as a responsible parent and failure to accept social norms with respect to lawful behavior. After age 30 the more flagrant aspects may diminish, particularly sexual promiscuity, fighting, criminality, and vagrancy."

Take two life sentences and call me in the morning.

Call them psychopaths, sociopaths, or antisocial person-alities—these are the people we think of as bad.

I will continue to call them *psychopaths*, because the term *antisocial personality disorder* is unwieldy, bland, and lends no more insight than did *sociopathy*. And because *psychopathy* has a nice, novelistic ring to it. It's a juicy term, connotative of evil, and this is a juicy, evil creature we're dealing with.

Let's take a closer look at the beast.

VI

Dissecting Evil

RESEARCHERS HAVE IDENTIFIED TWO DISTINCT components of psychopathy: the *impulsive* aspect, featuring lack of self-control and delay of gratification, failure to respond to long-term punishment, and high levels of sensation and thrill seeking (the fun of crime); and the *interpersonal* aspect, featuring inflated self-esteem, pathological lying, callousness, unemotionality, detachment, and lack of empathy (other people are garbage) (27).

The Book of Deuteronomy describes a "stubborn and rebellious son" whose incorrigible behavior merits death by stoning (28). Talmudic commentary clarifies that an actual case of incorrigibility meriting execution was improbable and, in fact, may have never occurred (29). Rather, the intention was to present a teaching case—a metaphorical warning of the danger that results when incorrigibility reaches dangerous proportions in a young person.

What is fascinating is how closely the elements that make up the stubborn and rebellious son match our contemporary understanding of psychopathy: extreme lust and gluttony (impulsive factors) and crime (interpersonal factors). Talmudic sages living two thousand years ago realized what some modern scholars have come to learn rather painfully: If extremes of bad behavior are not quelled very early in childhood, they are extremely difficult to reverse.

There are no actual data regarding rates of rehabilitation as they relate to age, but clinical experience has taught us that the older the child, the less pliable his behavior. The optimist in me wants to say, *Never give up on anyone*. But the chances of eliminating entrenched psychopathic behavior in an adolescent are extremely low, if not zero.

Nevertheless, it's important to examine the components of psychopathy in order to tease out how they impact upon crime. Young psychopaths are not a totally homogeneous group and vary in terms of where they fall along the impulsive and interpersonal dimensions. Those high in impulsivity are more likely to be explosive; those loaded on the latter tend to commit cold, cruel, premeditated crimes.

Further complicating the picture, there does exist a very small subset of psychopaths who display *schizoid* symptoms—schizophreniclike weirdness and extreme social isolation that approach but never reach full-blown madness. Schizoid psychopaths are violent hermits who act odd but understand what they are doing and possess the ability to plot, scheme, and evade capture. They are true psychological islands with no need whatsoever for intimacy or social connection. Even in prison they are feared and shunned, and they often exhibit the highest levels of cruelty.

Unabomber Theodore Kaczynski comes across as one of these evil isolates. His deviant behavior began in childhood. Bright enough to elude identification for decades, Kaczynski might very well have stretched his criminal career till the day of his death if his brother hadn't turned him in. As is typical of psychopaths, Kaczynski evinced no remorse and arrogantly attempted to justify his crimes using a combination of neo-Luddite and radical environmentalist pseudophilosophy. However, his writings reveal his primary motive to be hurting and killing other people. Fortunately, schizoid psychopaths are extremely rare—a minority among a minority.

Though variations in psychopathy do exist, psychopaths as a group are *less* variable than normal people. As one veteran detective once told me, "If you've met one career criminal, you've met 'em all. They're out of the cookie cutter."

This is certainly true of organized serial killers. As a crime novelist, I'm loath to admit this, but the Bundys and Gacys of this world are worlds away from brilliant, charmingly evil Hannibal Lecter. In fact, stripped of their lies and their evasions, real-life serial killers are flat, stereotypical, and downright *boring*— walking versions of Gertrude Stein's classic description of Oakland: There's no *there*, there.

How do they get that way?

No one knows, but two schools of thought have emerged along the same old ideological battle lines that have divided psychology—and its ancestors, philosophy and theology—since their inceptions as formal fields of study: *genetics versus environment.*

The nature-nurture tango probably dates back to the first curious human, but like most megaquestions, it remains an unanswerable parlor game. And like most dichotomies, the controversy has endured well past the point of usefulness. Time and time again, the most reasonable result of nature/nurture research turns out to be the middle ground: *Most human behavior is the result of the interaction between inborn traits and environment.* Scientists will continue to tease out specific proportions of acquired versus inborn influences because scientists are curious people and they need to publish articles in scholarly journals in order to achieve tenure. But these calculations have very little usefulness for public policy.

By point of illustration, let's say, purely hypothetically, that we discover criminality to be 30 percent environmentally related and 70 percent genetic. Where does this lead us proactively? Do we forget about child rearing and schooling because most bad behavior is inherited? Or do we redouble our efforts to improve the environment because 30 percent is a large chunk? Even if we opt to design programs, there's no reason to weigh them 30 percent toward environmental change to 70 percent toward genetic manipulation, because there's no reason to assume that proportion of cause has anything to do with proportion of optimal solution. The same would hold true if the environment played only a 10 percent role, because a tenth of something as important as criminality bears close attention.

Nevertheless, the nature/nurture debate rages within the pages of academic journals and on talk shows. And once again, "scientific" opinions are often influenced more by political attitudes and personal preconceptions than by facts.

Environmental determinism—the nurture side— has tended to be favored by those scholars who see themselves as social liberals, because belief in a strong governmental role in improving the quality of life depends upon the conviction that human behavior is tractable. Similarly, those mavens adhering to either libertarian or anarchic views that denigrate the role of government, or fiscally conservative ideologues with a jaundiced view of economic and social tinkering, are comfortable attributing human behavior to DNA-mediated brain chemistry because the resultant social pessimism goes a long way in justifying refusal to fund social programs.

Time and time again these two extreme views butt heads in the dreary corridors of government like a pair of deranged rams. When politics rears its ugly head, truth suffers.

But the average person understands. You don't need a Ph.D. or a think-tank job to figure it out.

It's both.

Does any reasonable person deny that environment strongly affects people? Or that inborn factors are a total wash? (Actually, during tumultuous times, ideological rigidity *can* lead to some pretty strange mental pretzels. When I was in graduate school during the early 1970s, radical feminist doctrine put forth the view that sex-role behaviors and attitudes—the visible manifestations of femininity and masculinity—were 100 percent learned: Give a boy a doll and he'll abandon cowboys and Indians, hand a girl a rifle and she'll grow up tough and macho. A brief visit to any newborn nursery would have dispelled this nonsense— even casual observation would have revealed differing rates of activity, muscularity, vocal pitch, and so on in the blue versus the pink bassinets. Ditto for the merest exposure to preschools, baby-sitting, or child rearing. But why let reality cloud your dogma?)

With regard to psychopathy, environmental theory has focused upon social factors such as poverty and abuse and psychological issues such as disruption of parent-child attachment, especially during the first two or three years of childhood. Studying the infant-toddler period makes intuitive good sense because much emotional conditioning occurs during this period and one of the most striking aspects of psychopathy is gross abnormality of the emotional system.

During early childhood, the foundations of interpersonal relationships are laid as the baby bonds with parents or caretakers by experiencing satiation of bodily needs, receiving physical and emotional nurturance, and learning to associate physical satisfaction with affection. Toddlers also develop specific strategies of coping with anger, fear, and frustration, and they begin to identify with other people at a rudimentary level and to reciprocate affection. The first signs of altruism and sympathy for others usually appear during toddlerhood, supplanting the infant's inborn narcissism.

Psychopaths make it to adulthood without ever developing the capacity for empathy and sympathy, though they learn to be quite good at imitating both. They view people as objects, which allows them to exploit, manipulate, and inflict high levels of pain on others without regret—what's wrong with cheating or stabbing a *thing*? It's not that they lack an understanding of morality and the rules of conduct—many psychopaths subscribe to some kind of moral code. In fact, imprisoned criminals often spout a strong law-and-order line. It's just that they believe the rules apply to others, not them.

Psychopaths are also quite enthusiastic about defending themselves physically—whether or not defense is necessary—and they display a heightened sense of inter-personal threat, perceiving aggression and hostility in the behavior of others when it doesn't exist (30). Like cornered animals, they are likely to lash out violently when they feel trapped.

Though calm, cool, and excellent sleepers, psycho-paths are by no means devoid of emotion. They experience anger and pleasure and boredom at high levels—indeed, they crave and often chase pleasure with a staggering single-mindedness. But anxiety, worry, and ambivalence are muted or absent, though the psychopath can mimic them—role playing of the most malignant variety.

Skillful, intelligent psychopaths can learn kindness, sensitivity, and morality as abstractions and weaknesses to be exploited, but they don't integrate these qualities into their personalities.

Psychopathy, like any other personality dimension, takes time to develop, and young killers such as Johnson and Golden can be thought of as incompletely fashioned criminals: impulsive, unsophisticated, lacking even the flawed judgment of adult psychopaths. Despite clear evidence of premeditation, as master felons the boys were pathetic duds—boasting about their intentions to anyone who'd listen, leaving behind mountains of evidence. No Sherlock was necessary to figure out whodunit. Lacking access to guns, their misdeeds would likely have expressed themselves as some variant of schoolyard bullying, perhaps a knifing.

Equipped with a firearms arsenal, their faulty reasoning, low impulse control, and lack of smarts had just the opposite result: mindless carnage.

It seems logical that disruption of the parent-child bonding process has something to do with this emotional warp. The problem is, the kind of data it would take to pinpoint how specific processes of emotional scrambling occur are hard to obtain, for we are generally unable to study and observe large numbers of children and family from the moment of birth through adulthood with the kind of detail necessary to establish causation. Some of the more thought-provoking studies about the biology of psychopathy have been produced in countries such as Sweden and Denmark, where national registries are maintained, but large-scale American data are conspicuously lacking.

One alternative to multigenerational longitudinal research involves studying kids who already exhibit high degrees of aggression, violence, and/or criminality and attempting to relate those characteristics to various measurements of early childhood disruption. Numerous studies have been carried out on the relationship between criminality and abuse, divorce and marital separation, and the intrusion of violence into the child's life, either directly or through the media.

Family breakdown, as exemplified by divorce and separation, is clearly related to a host of psychological problems in children, including school problems, truancy, alcoholism, and drug use, all of which are often precursors of criminal behavior. Childhood aggression seems to predict alcoholism and drug use in adolescence; in turn, substance abuse seems to predict adult criminality, especially when combined with parental alcoholism and drug use (5, 6, 31–33).

Seems to, because statistics are valid only for groups and are mathematically irrelevant when making predictions about individuals. Statistics can also be monkeyed with easily by experts in order to support whatever conclusions the researcher wants them to buttress.

One example of this is the misuse of a statistical concept commonly bandied about in the popular press: *correlation,* which is a mathematical expression of coexistence between two or more variables. *Correlation is not, by itself, causation.* Correlations simply state probability associations. A positive correlation means that when X is present, Y is more likely to be present. A negative correlation means the presence of X is more probable when Y is absent.

Correlations *can* be causal—smoking cigarettes is both correlated with and a cause of lung cancer. Putting a gun to one's head and pulling the trigger is highly correlated with, and causally linked to, infliction of a fatal wound.

But consider the correlation between blond hair and blue eyes. Both traits coexist at higher-than-chance rates, but neither trait brings about the other. Similarly, itching and wheezing resulting from exposure to an allergen are concomitant symptoms with a shared cause, but they lack a causal connection.

Another poorly understood statistic is the *power* of a correlation—how much variability within a group the correlation actually explains. Mathematically, this is obtained by squaring the correlation. By point of example, let's say we study the relationship between freckles and red hair in a group of people and come up with a correlation of +.60. This means that red-haired people tend to be freckled and vice versa (without saying anything about causality). However, there will also be plenty of red-haired people without freckles as well as freckled people without red hair (statisticians call this "scatter"). Squaring .60 (.60 × .60), we obtain .36, or 36 percent, which means that slightly over a third of the group can be classified as red-haired and freckled. That may still be important, but it's a long way from the majority status implied by the .60 correlation itself. Failure to understand the correlation-squared index is one reason nonscientists are often overly impressed by scientific data.

Given all these caveats, let's look at more of the data on environment and violence, criminality, and psychopathy.

Several studies of violent children, most of them based on small samples, indicate an extremely high degree of family chaos and child abuse in the backgrounds of kids who kill (9–13). Paternal absence is common, as are disproportionately high rates of fathers with a history of imprisonment and/or drug and alcohol abuse and/or psychopathy.

Fathers with a *specific* constellation of personality traits—high reactivity to stress, alienation, and aggression—seem to keep cropping up as progenitors of violent kids (32). The importance of paternal input makes sense when we remember that boys learn how to handle aggression from their fathers—or, when fathers are absent, from surrogate males, mainly peers, such as fellow gang members or mass-media figures. When one recalls that most violence is committed by males, the role of fathers looms especially large.

Of course, biological theorists would attribute these paternal factors to genetics: angry, alienated criminal men pass along their maladaptive traits to their sons. There is also information supporting the biological connection between gender and violence that bears consideration, specifically the well-known finding that the male sex hormone, testosterone, is positively related to levels of aggression, while the female hormone, estrogen, increases passivity.

All normal men and women have both chemicals coursing through their bloodstream, but testosterone is higher in men, and estrogen is higher in women. Even in women, levels of testosterone seem to make a difference: In a study of female prisoners, older inmates had lower testosterone levels and were less violent than younger cons (34).

Testosterone reaches its peak in adolescence and young adulthood and diminishes with age. Does this mean that a teenage psychopath fairly new to the crime game is actually more of a threat than a forty-five-year-old seasoned con? Not necessarily, because statistics say nothing about individuals, and individual factors play a large role in predicting violence. However, it is clear that as a *group*, young criminals—age seventeen through twenty-five—produce the highest rate of crime. Testosterone may be another reason, in addition to low impulse control and faulty judgment, why the crimes of young villains—urban gangbangers and teenage thrill killers—are often so horrifying, though it probably had little to do with Johnson and Golden, whose smooth, rosy-cheeked faces screamed prepubescence.

Diminishing levels of testosterone in middle age may also help explain a fascinating phenomenon: the tapering off of criminality observed in older psychopaths (35). This so-called *criminal burnout* is interesting in that what seems to be affected is the psychopath's energy level, not his soul. As psychopaths grow older, their impulsivity drops, as do their arrests. However, callousness and cruelty remain high. The same reduction of drive has been observed in heroin addicts lucky enough to survive into advanced middle age: Often the craving for the drug, previously impervious to any sort of treatment, simply vanishes on its own.

The bad guys stay bad, but they're too pooped to pop.

Whatever role biology plays, given what we know about the strength of imitative learning in children, it's not much of a logical leap to list role models who behave violently and who justify violence and aggression as valid problem-solving techniques as factors in child criminality. And today's kids, urban and suburban, are exposed to astoundingly high rates of actual violence (in one study, 90 percent of a sample of middle-school students from varying socioeconomic backgrounds reported knowing someone who'd been robbed, beaten, stabbed, shot, or murdered, and nearly 50 percent had been personally robbed, beaten up, stabbed, shot, or caught in gun crossfire) (36).

Another avenue of research along these lines has been the study of corporal punishment. It has been asserted that children disciplined physically are more likely to turn out violent than those who are controlled using "psychological" techniques such as withdrawal of attention and privileges. During the forties, the anthropologist Ashley Montagu went so far as to hyperbolize it this way: "Spanking the baby may be the psychological seed of war."

Several studies have shown a consistent association between corporal punishment and child aggression, criminality, and domestic violence (37). Recalling the distinction between correlation and causation, one might suggest, alternatively, that these findings have nothing to do with the deleterious effects of spanking per se.

Perhaps aggressive and violent children are spanked more because they misbehave more. Or that, once again, the mode of transmission is genetic—kids inherit patterns of violent behavior from violent parents, who are least likely to spare the rod.

But research into how children learn suggests that biology cannot completely explain away the association, and at least one longitudinal study that followed boys for thirty-three years found that while sons of fathers convicted of crimes were more likely to become criminals, *even when the paternal factor was eliminated statistically, the relationship between corporal punishment and criminality endured* (38). This makes perfect sense: Children identify with and imitate their parents and other caretakers in thousands of subtle and not-so-subtle ways. Why would aggression and violence be exceptions?

This is not to suggest that occasional spankings create murderers, but rather that a consistent pattern of beating to the virtual exclusion of other disciplinary techniques may teach the child the unhealthy lesson that violence works, in addition to preventing the development of guilt, shame, and conscience.

Think of the learning process that goes along with beating as a primary mode of behavior control, as opposed to disciplinary methods that guide the child toward self-examination and reflection ("Now, go to your room and *think* about what you did and why it's wrong"). Kids encouraged, urged, and pressured to reflect are being taught the foundations of morality. They are also being shown that misbehavior can be dealt with in ways other than through physical aggression.

Kids who are hit never go through this learning process. Corporal punishment tends to be swift and brutish. Typically, its recipients are smacked, punched, or kicked, then thrown back onto the streets like undersized fish. Case closed. There's no extended period in which to mull. The lesson absorbed by kids who are frequently beaten is that slugging someone is okay if you're big enough to get away with it.

"Might makes right" is the psychopath's first commandment.

The link between an outlook that justifies violence and actual violent behavior is supported by studies of aggressive boys who, when asked why hitting was wrong, tended to come up with answers involving the avoidance of punishment. Their less aggressive peers were more likely to focus upon the morality of violence.

There is also evidence that childhood violence is not a unitary concept, and that different types of aggression may result from different pathways.

One group of researchers studying boys who were aggressive at a very young age discerned two patterns of childhood violence that appeared to differ from each other with regard to family background (8).

The first group, termed *reactively aggressive*, consisted of youngsters exhibiting "hot-blooded" anger and hostile, violent rage brought about by perceived threat—the cornered-animal syndrome. When compared with nonaggressive kids, reactively aggressive youngsters tended to be highly impulsive and began to exhibit serious conduct problems from around the age of four. They were also more likely to have been harshly disciplined and abused at home, to come from poorer families, and to have experienced more family stress and problems with peers. These boys displayed more of the *impulsive* aspect of psychopathy.

In contrast was a scarier bunch, whose behavior displayed more of the *interpersonal* characteristics of psychopathy (callousness, cruelty). These were the *proactively aggressive* boys, youngsters who displayed a consistent pattern of highly organized, cold-blooded bullying and violence. They began misbehaving slightly later— at around six and a half—and appeared no different from nonaggressive boys in terms of environmental factors. In fact, *none* of these nasty little fellows was reported to have been abused.

However, these researchers used a highly questionable measurement of harsh discipline: asking the mother of both groups to describe any spanking or abuse. Since parents are unlikely to admit to beating their child, and especially not to extreme abuse that could result in criminal prosecution, this study may have grossly underestimated levels of punishment for the entire sample.

More important, the discrepancy may not have

been uniform, for if the cold-blooded, manipulative kids were more likely to have been raised by cold-blooded, manipulative mothers who lied more in order to cover up, their rates of abuse would have been disproportionately *under*reported.

Nevertheless, some other information from this study may shed some light on motivation for violence.

The hot-blooded kids were angry and poorly accepted by their peers and saw their aggressive behavior as a means of protecting themselves in a hostile, threatening world. The cold-blooded kids were more likely to talk about the *positive outcomes of violence*—to perceive aggression and hurting others as reliable and rewarding techniques for getting ahead in life. This protopsychopathic attitude may be the result of social learning—growing up in families and/or societies where the rewards of violence are high—or it may be a biological factor. Or both.

To the extent that this study does indicate genuinely higher levels of abuse in the hot-blooded kids, it's possible to theorize that kids from chaotic families who are beaten consistently develop a heightened sense of threat, as well as a repertoire of coping skills that emphasizes violence. This gives comfort to the liberal-environmentalist notion of the victim striking back.

Inconsistent with this model, of course, are the cold-blooded bullies with no apparent unusual stressors in their background who learn—or are born with—a tendency to believe that violence gets the goodies. The fact that cold-blooded boys start to show problems at a later age than the hot-blooded kids (six and a half versus four) might be seen as shifting the scales toward the environmentalist point of view, in that a genetic flaw might be expected to manifest itself earlier, not later. But this is not true. Genetic traits can make themselves apparent at any age. Perhaps the "defect" simply shows up around first grade.

If the cold-blooded boys were indeed not abused, does this mean they're born to be cruel?

Not necessarily. A social-learning approach would posit that, lacking the personal experience of being victimized, the cold-blooded kids are nonetheless picking up cues from nasty parents and disruptive surroundings that teach them it pays to hurt.

Other issues to consider when interpreting the role of corporal punishment and violence involve *degree* and *exclusivity*: How much spanking predisposes a child to aggression? More important, how strong is the association between even high levels of corporal punishment and subsequent adult criminality? The fact remains that while over 90 percent of American children are spanked, the vast majority do not turn into career criminals (37).

No definitive answer to these questions exists, but the most thorough epidemiologic studies of the connection between corporal punishment and overall violence in society have produced correlations in the .30

to .35 range. Using the correlation-squared formula, this leaves us with about a 9 or 10 percent loading.

A 10 percent contribution is important, but clearly other factors must be at play. Some of these variables may correlate with violent discipline, but others may be completely independent of it.

In addition to the previously noted biological factor—men with congenitally violent temperaments and other types of brain damage are more likely to beat their kids—environmental factors might include poverty, education, and social class. Many researchers have suggested that poorer children and those growing up in less educated households are beaten more often than are middle-class kids. In fact, many social theorists hold that poverty is the *most important* predictor of criminality, and hundreds of millions of dollars have been spent studying and attempting to remedy the issue.

Unfortunately, the data do not support the primacy of poverty as a predictor of violence. Though crime rates are higher in poor communities and hot-blooded violence is somewhat associated with lower socioeconomic status, the vast majority of poor people are not criminals, nor is there any indication that poverty leads to the most frightening types of cold, cruel crimes committed by violent, career psychopaths. Furthermore, poverty statistics as they relate to crime may be misleading because, lacking the resources for escape and defense, poorer criminals may be more likely to be caught and convicted of felonies.

A well-run, large-scale study of mostly poor, inner-city kids found that while some of the life stresses associated with poverty correlated with antisocial behavior (at relatively low levels), poverty per se did not (39). This is also consistent with clinical interviews of incarcerated criminals by researcher Samuel Yochelson and Stanton Samenow, who discovered that, contrary to the notion that felons steal and rob because they lack the opportunity to earn money legally, a surprising number of cons possess excellent job skills and talents that they *choose* not to exploit because they are lazy, believe themselves too wonderful to have to work, and perceive crime as their profession (40). Recall thirteen-year-old Tim's early "business" dealings, complete with engraved calling cards.

Yochelson and Samenow also discovered that some criminals maintained steady employment as a means of *enhancing* their criminality, one example being the air-conditioning repairman who used maintenance calls as an opportunity to case the homes in which he worked.

The issue of race as it relates to psychopathy also bears mention. Approximately 45 percent of inmates in U.S. prisons are black, a figure that is approximately four times the rate of blacks in the general population. The notion that blacks have a biologically determined higher rate of criminality and/or psychopathy is laden with racist overtones and is sure to be met with anger and counterclaims that black crime is primarily a reaction to oppression (a special subset of hot-blooded aggression). A study comparing black and white inmates offers some support for this, but it also suggests that psychopathy is a good predictor of criminality when applied to blacks as well as whites (41).

These researchers, using the most widely accepted and reliable test of psychopathy, the Hare Psychopathy Checklist, found that black psychopaths showed more similarities than dissimilarities to their white brethren. And for both black and white convicts, psychopathy was positively associated with violence as adults. Furthermore, in a related study of the same inmate sample, black psychopaths exhibited some of the same distinctive learning problems displayed by white psychopaths.

However, important differences also emerged. All the raters in the study were white, and they judged black prisoners to be more psychopathic than white prisoners, raising the suspicion that racism and/or unfamiliarity with black culture contribute to an "overpathologization" of blacks. Supporting this is the finding that black psychopaths are less similar to whites on certain core factors of the *interpersonal* aspect of psychopathy—callousness, cruelty, glibness, tendency to lie—but much more consistent on impulsive items pertaining to an *unstable, poorly socialized lifestyle*. In addition, for blacks, the Hare test didn't discriminate cleanly between interpersonal and impulsive factors, suggesting, again, that cultural bias may have influenced the psychopathy ratings.

Overall, these results indicate that while the concept of psychopathy shouldn't be abandoned when studying black criminals, standard tests of psychopathy may be measuring different factors in blacks and whites, with the former perhaps more influenced by "hot-blooded" elements related to abuse and poverty.

Ironically, a social-liberal approach could theoretically be more comfortable with the idea that blacks exhibit higher rates of psychopathy, for if antisocial behavior is nothing more than a learned reaction to oppression, blacks, a group clearly subjected to more racism and socioeconomic deprivation than whites, could be *expected* to be more psychopathic. And if family breakdown is a causal factor for psychopathy, the fact that 95 percent of black teenage mothers are unwed bears some serious notice. (Though, with a 65 percent rate, white and Hispanic girls aren't far behind.)

Whatever the statistical specifics, we should not be deterred from identifying and segregating severe psychopaths of any ethnicity. Whether a cold, cruel, habitual criminal is black, white, yellow, Jewish, Christian, or Buddhist is of little solace to his victims. The fact remains that once he's locked up for a long time, the rest of us will be safer.

The most reasonable conclusion that can be drawn about environment and psychopathy is that some combination of environmental stressors—physical abuse, social chaos, parental drug use and alcoholism, and overall rotten families, especially rotten and/or absent fathers—contributes to severe antisocial behavior in young boys. In many cases this develops into psychopathy and a lifetime of criminality.

VII

The Scapegoat We Love to Hate

SOCIAL PROBLEMS MAY REQUIRE LONG-TERM solutions, but that shouldn't deter us from seeking efficient, short-term solutions to severe juvenile crime. If increased public safety is our goal, efficiency also dictates that we cease pouring money into research and clinical activities that have little direct impact upon rates of child criminality. A prime example of such diminished returns is the flood of studies conducted on the factor most often blamed for childhood criminality: *media violence.*

Each time another "senseless" crime involving a young criminal hits the news, one reaction is certain: a spate of editorials blaming the outrage—and the downfall of society in general—on rising levels of violence portrayed on television, motion pictures, and video games.

This is nothing new. During the pioneering days of radio, panic calls were sounded about the deleterious effects of radio crime shows upon American youth (42). And there is no doubt that children do have the opportunity to avail themselves of more vicarious violence than in previous generations (though it might be argued that boys drafted into the wars that preoccupied America during the previous two and half centuries were exposed to a good deal more *real* violence than are today's virtual warriors).

Numerous studies have produced correlations and other statistical associations between media violence and aggression in children (43). Explanations include (1) *sanitization and desensitization*—after repeated exposure to violence, kids get used to witnessing cruelty and mayhem and grow less loath to use it; (2) *identification*—kids imitate whatever they see on-screen; (3) *arousal*—kids are unhealthily stimulated by media violence and perceive it as thrilling and something to be tried; and (4) *positive reinforcement*—kids learn from TV and the movies that violence is rewarded.

Though some statistical support has been obtained for all four suppositions, *not a single causal link between media violence and criminality has ever been produced.*

Part of the reason for the failure to establish causation may be methodological: Television and motion picture viewing are ubiquitous—virtually every child in America and other Western cultures watches oodles of TV, so it is difficult to come up with control groups and to otherwise tease out specific effects of media violence. For that reason, most prospective media studies have taken place in laboratory settings where children are exposed to media images and then tested, using paper-and-pencil questionnaires or interviews, on their attitudes about violence and aggressiveness.

The problem with this approach is one that plagues social science research in general: laboratory experiments and field ("real-life") studies have proven notoriously inconsistent. In fact, in certain areas of psychological inquiry, such as attitude change, results from lab research are often the *opposite* of those obtained by field studies, with the former concluding that attitudes are comparatively easy to modify while the latter find them resistant to change.

Lab/field discrepancies may be due to the artificial nature of the experimental setting: The experimenter overly controls the situation by projecting an air of authority that leads the subject to respond in a certain manner. In addition, the attitudes and behaviors measured in the lab are often constructed to be experimentally "clean"—unrelated to prior prejudices and relatively value-free. Unfortunately, this also means they have little or no relevance to the experimental subjects. It is fairly easy to change one's opinion about some trivial construct created by Professor Gadget, and quite another matter to modify one's deeply ingrained views on race and religion.

Another problem with media violence research

involves applicability. Do the results of a questionnaire about some theoretical situation involving risk taking or aggressive problem solving filled out by a child who's just watched a violent cartoon have anything to do with real-life aggressiveness, let alone psychopathy or criminality?

Further clouding the issue are contradictory data, such as a lack of evidence of rising crime rates in comparatively nonviolent societies, such as Japan, following the introduction of TV, and the fact that the highest rates of recorded violence in today's world are found in regions, such as Latin America and Africa, where television viewing is *lower* than it is in the United States.

Yet other findings bring us back to the old correlation/causation snafu: Both degree of exposure and reactions to the violent images portrayed by TV and film appear to *interact* with the traits and characteristics that the child brings into the viewing situation.

For example, it has been found that highly aggressive boys watch more TV than nonaggressive boys and that they are affected more by what they see (44). This may be due to their lack of creativity and subsequent need for "canned" stimulation. It is also consistent with biological notions of psychopaths as chronically, physiologically understimulated emotional paupers who lack rich mental imagery and chase sensation.

Another reason high-risk boys may be the ones mostly attracted to the easy, passive stimulation provided by the visual media may be *parental incompetence.*

We know that many violent kids are more likely to grow up in chaotic, neglectful, and abusive households, and to be exposed to drug and alcohol abuse. Perhaps the poorly raised boy, allowed to play hooky and to veg out at home, stoned or drunk, simply has more time available to sit glued to the tube.

Yet another potential complication is the possibility that children who grow up in the rotten households that practice and glamorize violence may be more likely to regard the violent imagery they see on the screen as comfortingly familiar. If so, the media are playing a reinforcing role rather than a generative one. While this is certainly harmful, it is the chaotic family that we should be addressing, rather than the media.

The importance of considering temperament, traits, and personality characteristics as they interact with media violence cannot be overemphasized. Let me offer a totally unscientific, but I believe instructive, example from my personal experience.

I have four children, three of whom are old enough to have viewed many popular violent movies, including numerous horror films. My eldest daughter, in particular, displayed an early attraction to motion pictures full of images I found disgusting and shocking. My wife and I were reluctant to let her watch these bloody flicks, but my daughter insisted they wouldn't harm her. Since she'd always been a delightful girl, we relented . . . and watched for problems. None followed. My eldest daughter passed through the splatter-flick phase and moved on to new fare. Never did she exhibit a trace of violence or antisocial behavior as a consequence of what she saw. Never did I observe *any* side effect of viewing, and this shrink dad was *looking* for symptoms. Years later, my eldest daughter remains an honor student and one of the sweetest, least violent people I've ever met.

My son and my second daughter never developed any idiosyncratic interest in violent films, but simply by being teenagers in contemporary America, they too were exposed to violence and gore at a level much more explicit than what I grew up with.

I recall viewing the classic Hitchcock film *Psycho* in my late teens and leaving the theater absolutely petrified. At its initial release, *Psycho* was considered a revolutionary film primarily because it ratcheted screen violence up several notches. Adults were terrified by the images Hitchcock purveyed, especially the famous shower stabbing scene. Some viewers were even reported to have experienced heart attacks.

When my three oldest watched *Psycho*—as *early* adolescents—the film barely raised their eyebrows, so mild did they find it compared to *Nightmare on Elm Street, Friday the 13th, Halloween,* and others.

Personal anecdotes are not scientific. But the absolute lack of effect upon my progeny of violent media images remains in stark contrast to all the warnings promulgated by would-be media-blamers. Yes, desensitization definitely occurred in my kids—lowering their anxiety about screen violence but not real-life violence—and I suspect the same is true of tens of millions of other kids, because while nearly all American children watch violent movies and TV, only a very minute percentage becomes criminal.

This is not to say media violence is harmless. To the extent that gory junk attracts high-risk youngsters, it's anything but. Is it possible that an already psychopathic boy with a head full of violent impulses that have festered since early childhood, sitting around the house sucking on a joint or sniffing glue while he watches *Scream*, can be spurred to imitate what he sees on the screen? Absolutely.

The same is true of printed violence—serial killers often collect violent pornography and true-crime magazines in order to heighten sexual arousal. But for these psychopaths, print images are used to stimulate associations between sexuality and violence that are already well developed. The overwhelming majority of people who read pornography and true-crime magazines are not serial killers, nor do they become serial killers because of what they encounter between the covers of *Shocking Detective*.

Given no bloody books, no Freddy Krueger on video, no thrash metal or gangsta rap, would Billy Rotten of bullying, cat-mutilating proclivities have picked up a knife and stabbed his mother anyway? No way to know for sure, but I'd bet yes. And the likelihood of Billy's engaging in serious violence somewhere along the line would remain extremely high no matter what he read or viewed, because the variables that strongly influence violent behavior are likely to be a lot more personal than those elicited by wielding the remote control.

Even granting that media violence affects some kids negatively, what can be done to fix the problem?

The best solution is obviously to have parents exercise good judgment and restrict access to nasty material in the case of a child who shows tendencies toward violence. But failure to limit TV is way at the bottom of the list of parental inadequacies experienced by high-risk kids.

We are certainly unlikely to put in place the large-scale solution that might partially handle the problem—widespread censorship foisted upon 99.9 percent of the population in order to shield a tiny minority—because that type of group punishment is antagonistic to our democratic norms, not to mention unconstitutional. And I emphasize *partially*, because any kind of blanket prohibition of violent films and shows will inevitably result in a black market of forbidden images, with those we are trying to shield most likely to get their hands on illegal goods.

A thorough and well-thought-out review of media violence and children summed it up wisely: "Aggression as a problem solving behavior is learned early in life, is usually learned well, and is resistant to change. Individual variation in the level of aggressive behavior and violence in children, adolescents and adults depends on many interacting factors of which media influences are likely to be less important than constitutional, parental, educational and other environmental influences. Contributing factors include being the victims of violence and bullying and witnessing violence perpetrated against others, especially at home. The emphasis on establishing whether television violence and actual violence are related has resulted in the neglect of these other, more important influences on the development of aggressive behaviors" (45).

Nevertheless, railing against the media is likely to continue as the knee-jerk response to child criminality because it is the type of facile, glib "explanation" that is perfectly in sync with today's short-attention-span journalism, and because it offends no constituency other than a small group of network executives and moguls. Using the media as a whipping boy is also extremely attractive to that most superficial and insincere group of "experts"—politicians—because it lends itself to sound bites and generates funding for the scores of do-nothing legislative commissions that pass for problem-solving units in a bureaucracy.

Though essentially a dead-end topic, media violence is likely to endure as a fruitful source of research grants for social scientists, producing much more heat than light about the causes and fixes of criminal violence.

VIII

The Biology of Being Bad

DURING OUR DISCUSSION OF ENVIRONMENTAL factors, biology has crept in often, because, as noted, the distinction between nature and nurture is artificial. Nevertheless, a number of studies do exist that have attempted to isolate organic variables, and they deserve attention.

Biological explanations for psychopathic (and all types of deviant) behavior are frightening, because biological determinism seems to fly in the face of concepts such as free will and social rehabilitation, and it raises the terrifying specter of the immutable "bad seed."

More important, serious abuses of biological determinism have been frequent and nightmarish, leading to such repellent outrages as eugenics—the pseudoscience of "cleansing" the human race through selective breeding, developed by the brilliant but misguided (and sterile) nineteenth-century British mathematician Francis Galton—and its philosophical offspring: forced sterilization, euthanasia, and genocide. Genetic dominance of intelligence and other traits has long been a pet cause of xenophobes and racists. The Nazi Holocaust had its roots in eugenics theory.

Another risk when evaluating biological research is the intellectual seductiveness of apparently hard science. It is easy to overvalue studies crammed with chemical compounds, graphs, and equations because they appear to offer authoritative, relatively clear-cut answers to complex questions, especially when compared to the fuzzy conundrums produced by social science research. But what looks like incontrovertible science often turns out to be no more than supposition and guesswork overlaid with a veneer of quantitative data. Just as is true of its softer cousin, "hard" science is profoundly vulnerable to the value judgments and prejudices of its all-too-fallible practitioners. The same methodological problems that often scrape the blush from the first fruits of social science data can apply equally to biological studies. Cautions such as our old friend *Correlation ain't necessarily causation* are just as valid.

Nevertheless, nearly five decades of research on the biological aspects of psychopathy and criminality have produced some provocative data that deserve to be addressed.

And though we must examine biological data critically, we needn't be scared off by some brave-new-world threat of genetic determinism, because while some biological phenomena are genetically based, *many others are not.*

In fact, the distinction between genetics and biology is a prime example of the correlation/causation caveat appropriately applied: Simply because something manifests itself on a cellular, hormonal, or biochemical level does not mean its *origins* are based in inborn cellular, hormonal, or biochemical processes.

Put simply, biology modifies environment, but environment also modifies biology.

Consider the example of identical (monozygotic) twins—pairs of siblings endowed with identical DNA. Most identical twins resemble each other strongly, yet individual sets of twins differ greatly in their degree of identicality. Some are almost completely identical, while others display significant physical and behavioral differences. Most important, *no identical twins are absolute carbon copies of each other.*

I am personally familiar with identical twins, young women, one of whom is two inches taller than her sister. Height is to a great extent determined by genes, but even here the causal pathway is clearly not 100 percent genetic.

What nongenetic (but biological) factors might have played a role in the two-inch discrepancy? Perhaps as fetuses these women underwent specific intrauterine experiences that affected their respective heights, with one twin lucking into a superior position within the womb—a literal upper hand—that provided her with the lion's share of placental nutrition and movement, simultaneously restricting her sibling's snacks and aerobic exercise. Or maybe postnatal experiences, such as illness and injury, intervened.

We needn't limit ourselves to twins when searching for examples of the discontinuity between biological and genetic causality. Average heights and weights of Japanese citizens and those of other developing nations increased significantly following World War II, due to changes in nutrition.

With regard to children, a variety of prenatal insults that have nothing to do with chromosomes can strongly affect growth and subsequent development. Youngsters exposed to maternal malnutrition and injury, as well as to alcohol, tobacco, and other toxins, are more likely to evince brain damage, birth defects, learning problems—and antisocial behavior—than are nonpoisoned controls. The same goes for birth complications, prematurity, and postnatal damage, such as poisoning by lead chips in old paint, head trauma, infections, and recurrent fevers.

Several studies of child and adult murderers indicate high rates of brain damage as measured by learning disabilities, attention deficit, school problems, EEG (brain wave) measurement, and low IQ, but whether or not any of these deficits is genetic is unclear (9–13, 46).

In some cases, such as documented episodes of cranial injury, they certainly are not. And given strong evidence that many psychopaths and criminals are more likely to be abused, it's not much of a stretch to connect early maltreatment, such as kicks to the head, to environmentally caused brain damage.

Before we jump on brain damage as a defense, however, it's important to realize that the data on cerebral pathology and adult criminality are suggestive but not close to definitive. Some studies of psychopathic criminals have failed to produce strong evidence of brain abnormality (47). Nevertheless, a host of information does seem to indicate consistent differences between psychopaths and normal people that point to some kind of biological irregularity, possibly in the anterior (front) part of the brain, a region implicated in the regulation of emotion, reasoning, and social aggression.

Most conspicuously, psychopaths appear to exhibit *lower physiological arousal* than do normal individuals. This fits with the long-documented observation that psychopathic criminals fail to display fear and anxiety in situations that upset normal people, and seem to have great difficulty learning from unpleasant experiences. They also appear to be underresponsive to emotional stimuli in general. The notion of the stone-cold killer is based in reality (48, 49).

Some specific examples: When a sample of emotionally disturbed adolescents in treatment was divided on the basis of sleep patterns, the poor sleepers were more likely to be neurotic, while the sound sleepers tended to be psychopathic (15). A study of the level of stress hormone in the urine of arrested men showed increased secretion in nonpsychopaths as trial date approached, but no such pattern in psychopaths (22). Psychopaths have consistently shown lack of fear when exposed to frightening stimuli, though, as noted, they are quite vigilant about sensing threat and responding with anger (21). Most troubling is that these tendencies show themselves during early childhood.

Two theories have attempted to explain the connection between a cold nervous system and criminality. The first, *disinhibition,* emphasizes fearlessness. Relatively unburdened by anxiety, the psychopath fails to respond to the threat of punishment and engages in risky behaviors that draw him into antisocial activities. And indeed, psychopaths often do act in an eerily calm, unflustered manner when doing things that would terrify and shock the rest of us. Ted Bundy continued to smile, mug for the cameras, and lie convincingly throughout his arrest, imprisonment, and trial, with the mask beginning to crack only as execution drew near.

Strikingly realistic depictions of the blithe psychopath can be found more readily in fiction than in the psychiatric literature, with writers such as Elmore Leonard, Jim Thompson, Ruth Rendell, Charles Willeford, and my wife, Faye Kellerman (check out her novel *Justice*), capturing this persona with astonishing clarity. Lou Ford, Thompson's glib, emotionally flat, and pseudoinnocent sheriff protagonist of *The Killer Inside Me*, may very well be *the* perfect portrait of unruffled evil.

The second approach to underreactivity, *sensation seeking*, posits that chronically low levels of brain stimulation cause the psychopath to embark on a constant search for thrills. And indeed, psychopaths often do display very low thresholds for boredom, as well as high rates of alcohol and drug abuse that can be viewed as intense sensation-seeking behavior, or even self-medication for chronic mental emptiness.

The variables most commonly used to quantify arousability as it relates to antisocial behavior have been heart rate, skin conductance (the level of electrical activity passing along the skin, often related to perspiration), and brain wave patterns. Ironically, the first two are also components of the polygraph, the so-called lie detector—an apparatus whose practical value is based upon the premise that uttering falsehoods produces bodily arousal. But if psychopaths are indeed *less* arousable than normal people, they could be expected to beat the machine at higher rates than the rest of us. Furthermore, if there is a direct relationship between degree of psychopathy and "coolness"—the more psychopathic, the less flappable—then those criminals most likely to render the polygraph useless may very well be the most pathological and dangerous liars.

The findings of arousability research are anything but clear-cut. Skin conductance studies have produced inconsistent results: Some researchers have found a relationship between psychopathy and low skin conductance; others have not (50). Fogging the matter further, no consistent relationship has been found between skin conductance and criminality per se. So if a link between skin conductance and deviance does exist, it appears to explain only antisocial *tendencies* rather than the actual *commission* of misdeeds.

Brain wave research, as noted, has produced mixed results in the opposite direction. There is plenty of evidence that institutionalized criminals—children, adolescents, and adults—display higher rates of learning and attentional problems as well as EEG abnormality (though EEG findings are notoriously difficult to interpret), but no consistent irregularities have been identified in psychopaths (9–13, 51, 52).

Heart rate appears somewhat more promising. Numerous studies have shown that antisocial individuals exhibit significantly lower cardiac arousability than do normal persons, as measured by relatively low resting heart rates as well as cardiac systems that fail to respond strongly to threatening situations (50, 53). Heart rate, as Adrian Raine, the most prolific researcher in this area, has stated, is the "strongest and best replicated finding in the field of the psychophysiology of antisocial behavior"(50). However, once again, as Raine himself points out, the link seems to be to psychopathy, not criminality. Prisons are full of people with normal and hyperactive nervous systems.

Part of the problem may be that most heart rate research has been retrospective—selecting a sample of adult psychopaths or criminals and measuring their arousability. This tells us nothing about any developmental or causal process, nor does it control for confounding factors. For example, we know that heart rate decreases steadily throughout childhood, reaching its low point around the age of twenty, before reversing and commencing a gradual rise that may continue throughout adulthood. So perhaps studies of grown-up criminals have missed the boat. Certainly research that doesn't take age into account should be considered questionable.

In response to these problems, Raine and his colleagues, as well as others, have carried out *prospective* studies, measuring cardiac arousability in very young children and following these youngsters into adolescence and adulthood (54–56). This work was conducted in countries with well-established, centralized systems of socialized medicine that allowed access to large-scale data banks, primarily Scandinavia and the United Kingdom, as well as in isolated, easily studied communities such as the tiny Indian Ocean island of Mauritius. So cultural differences may limit the relevance of these studies to American society. But their results are striking and deserve more than casual attention.

The Mauritius Child Health Study, conducted by Raine and his associates, is especially noteworthy because every child on the island born in 1969 was studied at the age of three, providing a sample of 1,795 (later reduced to 1,130 after a cyclone destroyed many of the island's homes) (54). Heart rate was studied and measures of psychological adjustment were taken eight years later. The basic finding was that low resting cardiac rate in toddlers predicted aggressiveness and antisocial tendencies at a better-than-chance level even when environmental factors, such as social deprivation and broken homes, and biological factors, such as body size, activity level, physical development, muscle tone, and general health, were controlled for.

Research carried out by Raine also approached the issue from the opposite end, suggesting the protective nature of arousability. In these studies, youngsters at high risk for criminality because they had criminal fathers were more likely to *avoid* crime if their resting heart rates during childhood were high. Fear, it appears, can be a highly effective teacher (55–57).

Nevertheless, these findings lead us to the same kinds of problems we faced when assessing environmental variables: Assuming a link exists between cardiac activity and antisocial behavior, *how important is it and what does it mean?* A better-than-chance prediction rate may be fine when submitting a paper or playing blackjack, but what practical ramifications does it have for the amelioration of childhood violence? Is anyone suggesting that we segregate preschool kids simply on the basis of low heart rates, offering them antidelinquency training because of their EKG profiles? Even if this were socially acceptable or feasible, it wouldn't be wise because we'd be wasting plenty of time preaching to kids who didn't need it while failing to detect a good number of criminals-in-training. Heart rate studies reveal plenty of boys with normal heart rates who subsequently become aggressive, antisocial, even criminal, as well as low-heart-rate kids who don't turn bad.

Raine himself may have provided some clarity when he reported that a *combination* of birth complications, maternal rejection, and low arousability was the best predictor of serious violence in Danish children (58, 59). So optimal protection against criminality may result from environmental factors, such as a mother who takes care of herself during pregnancy and stays married to a nonviolent father in order to maintain an intact, loving family, rather than from a few more heartbeats per minute.

Yet another insulator against criminality is intelligence, which has been shown to be strongly negatively correlated with violence, even in children with low arousability and troubled backgrounds. However, there is some evidence that when bright boys from intact homes *do* turn bad, the link with underarousal is especially strong (50). One thinks of Leopold and Loeb dispassionately plotting the abduction and murder of Bobby Frank as an intellectual exercise, or the Menendez brothers retreating to the driveway of the family mansion in order to reload their shotguns.

So it's possible that there exists a small number of children, physiologically predisposed to antisocial behavior at a very young age, for whom a too-quiet nervous system *is* such a strong behavioral pollutant that it overrides environment. Are these kids true bad seeds, predestined genetically to evil? Or is underarousal not an inborn trait at all, but a *learned response* to abuse and neglect—a switching off of the child's nervous system in an effort to blunt psychic and physical pain?

Even the sterling facade of an intact, intelligent family may camouflage severe emotional neglect and horrendous maltreatment. (This was the Menendez brothers' precise defense, and it almost worked, despite a total lack of evidence. The circumstances of the murder certainly don't indicate defensive rage; at the time of her murder, Mrs. Menendez was performing the abusive act of filling out Erik's UCLA parking application. And several facts of the case—the glibness with which Lyle and Erik protested their innocence, the calculated nature of their crimes, subsequent attempts to deflect suspicion, the rapidity with which they began spending their dead parents' money on Porsches and Rolexes—indicate more than a bit of psychopathy.)

Whether or not the Menendez brothers' defense was nothing more than a creative bit of lawyering—my biases are obvious—is beside the point. What did or didn't occur in the house on North Elm Drive doesn't change what I learned early as a psychologist: lifting affluent and middle-class family rocks can reveal some truly revolting stuff. So much for the notion that poverty causes crime.

We know that many abused kids are more likely to exhibit a specific constellation of psychological problems known as *dissociative reactions*—symptoms such as withdrawal, amnesia, and, in extreme cases, multiple personality—which involve a literal partitioning of the mind, separating one's reality into protectively independent segments. Debate rages within psychiatry and psychology as to whether or not these symptoms represent true pathology or some sort of role playing, but either way, dissociation remains an attempt to shut out horror. Perhaps other victims of child abuse adopt a similar method of self-defense—a turning down of the emotional thermostat that cools and comforts by creating a sort of psychic cryogenics.

The nature of adolescence as it relates to abuse, changes in arousability, and violence also deserves attention. The concomitance of peaks in criminal violence and low heart rate between the ages of fifteen and twenty is striking. During this period, the teenager's body is being subjected to hormonal fluctuations and physiological changes that can turn adolescence into a

period of serious emotional upheaval. Even for normal, well-nurtured, well-adjusted kids, the teen years
can be tumultuous, rife with extremes of moodiness,
insecurity, narcissism, and an often stumbling trajec-
tory toward independence and autonomy. As any parent knows, even the brightest teenagers often exhibit
incredibly stupid behaviors—situational idiocy that tran-
scends mere IQ. How much more chaotic is the transi-
tion to sexual and physical maturation in abused kids?

Perhaps the process goes something like this: Some
of the formerly powerless, vulnerable, maltreated children who survive to adolescence by numbing down
their autonomic nervous systems find that same system
suddenly tweaked and supercharged by testosterone
and in dire need of sensual stimulation. One quick
avenue of satisfaction is drugs, hence the strong and
consistent relationship between narcotics and alcohol
abuse and psychopathy and criminality. In fact, drugs
play a role on both ends—as cause *and* effect—for in
addition to satisfying pleasure drives, psychoactive
chemicals lower inhibitions, facilitating risky, reckless,
sometimes psychopathic behavior. When booze and
dope fail to satisfy the cravings, the once-numb, now
pleasure-craving adolescent may turn elsewhere, including to the power and kick of crime. Having been
denied empathy and compassion, he lacks the capacity
and the desire to reciprocate with either. He's learned a
long time ago that victimizing others is an effective
way to obtain what you want if you're sufficiently big,

strong, and duplicitous to get away with it. Hungry to satisfy inchoate but compelling needs, he goes out and takes what he wants.

Empirical support for the numbing hypothesis as a consequence of emotional deprivation comes from a study that found children whose parents divorced by age four had lower resting heart rates at age eleven than did youngsters from intact homes (60). And the phenomenon may not be unique to humans: Adrian Raine cites research with fetal rats indicating a link between emotional stress and changes in the frontal lobes of the brain—the area most often implicated in aggressive behavior in humans (61).

More directly applicable to child criminality, a study measuring dangerousness in a group of delinquents found a triad of factors to be strongly predictive of violence: psychopathy, low IQ, and love deprivation, with *the last the single most potent factor.* Teenagers in whom all three were present were *over four times as likely* to engage in violent crime as any other comparison group (62).

In fact, Adrian Raine, the preeminent researcher on the psychophysiology of violence, is quick to suggest that the coldness exhibited by psychopaths may very well be a learned response to very early trauma (50). Rather than adopt a biologically deterministic model of human behavior, Raine wisely opts for what he terms a "biosocial" approach in which environmental stress causes actual changes in brain chemistry.

Nature? Nurture? It's both.

The numb-child-becomes-angry-adult scenario may also be consistent with the finding that parents who abuse their children show *high* arousability. We know that abused kids are more likely to become abusive parents, so some of these adults may once have been emotionally suppressed victims who now find themselves in the power role and undergo the transformation to hot-blooded victimizer. Since emotional arousability reaches its low point around the age of twenty, we would expect any upward shift to occur in early adulthood—precisely when most individuals are raising children.

Yet another indication of the biopsychosocial nature of low arousability is the fact that adult psychopaths are by no means uniformly cool. As mentioned, they show higher attentiveness to perceived threat and are more likely to react defensively and violently. And though they tend to tune out neutral and fearful stimuli, they can be hyperattentive to matters that interest them (63).

The bottom line regarding biological predictors of aggression, violence, and criminality is that a genuine link most likely *does* exist between underarousability, as measured by heart rate, and some kinds of psychopathy, but we are a long way from specifying either the precise nature or the strength of the relationship.

IX

It's Both

F ROM A PRACTICAL STANDPOINT, A *combination* of temperament and chaotic environment is by far the best predictor of dangerousness in children, just as it is in adults.

The strongest empirical support for the interaction between environmental and biological damage comes from studies of children and teenagers who've actually killed. Features found repeatedly in young murderers include language disorders suggestive of brain damage; a history of physical and sexual abuse; exposure to frequent, high-level, real-life episodes of extreme violence, primarily within the family; other indications of family chaos, most notably parental promiscuity, incarceration, and substance abuse; low IQ (90 or below); serious school problems; alcohol and drug abuse (mostly cocaine); and documented instances of head trauma. (I will examine later how Mitchell Johnson and Andrew Golden fit into this picture.)

A study of fourteen juveniles who committed sexual homicide—youths ranging from thirteen to seventeen years old who stalked, raped, stabbed, impaled, and mutilated their victims—revealed a similar set of precursors: violent, chaotic, abusive families; paternal abandonment or neglect; school problems and truancy; substance abuse; and attention deficit hyperactivity disorder. What separated these youths from other killers, much as it distinguishes adult sexual psychopaths from other criminals, was an early preoccupation with violent erotic fantasies. Media violence did play a role in the behavior of two members of this tiny subgroup, but it appears to have been minimal: one young rapist-murderer with long-festering violent impulses reported being inspired by a video game *(Dungeons and Dragons)*, and another linked his method, stabbing in the head, but not his fantasies, to the movie *Rambo* (13).

One contrast between these young lust-murderers and other precocious killers was their higher intelligence (mean group IQ was 101.4). This same "criminal intellectuality" is also found in many organized adult serial killers, many of whom tend to score above average on IQ tests. So these precocious lust-slayers may very well have been bush-league Ted Bundys who, fortunately for the rest of us, lacked the sophistication to avoid early capture.

X

Warning Signs and Solutions

I T IS VERY RARE FOR teen murderers to be good kids who suddenly turn bad. The exception is a subgroup of abused children who lash out defensively against their tormentors, behavior that might be considered self-defense. However, a study of teens who murdered family members found only a small proportion of killers to be reacting against abuse. On the contrary, rather trivial events, such as being refused the family car, were more common triggers (64).

Youths who murder strangers and family members who did not abuse them typically exhibit marked and consistent signs of violence and criminality long before taking life. Recurrent factors are fascination with weapons, carrying guns and knives to school, engaging in frequent fights, cruelty to animals, and sexual solicitation of young girls. Most child murderers have also been arrested before, often several times, with common prior offenses being burglary, robbery, assault, battery, grand theft, and trespassing.

And, much like Andrew Golden, Mitchell Johnson, and nearly every other boy who's chosen to shoot up a school, the young killers studied by scientists tend to have been anything but closemouthed about criminal intent. Many joked, boasted, or warned explicitly of their plans to commit rape and homicide.

No one took them seriously. Why? Probably because our romanticization of childhood leads us to doubt the possibility that any child can be a premeditated slayer.

It shouldn't.

As a psychologist, I especially should have known better than to be shocked by the massacre carried out by Andrew Golden and Mitchell Johnson, because ethically and morally, kids are works in progress. Throw in psychopathy and you've got a soul that will never be complete. Add access to weapons, and what else can you expect *but* tragedy?

Childhood violence has always been a problem. Historically, many societies have channeled the murderous urges of the young by drafting kids into the military. This practice continues in many Third World cultures; American soldiers in Vietnam have recounted the shock of coming up against platoons of prepubescent guerrillas.

Sometimes military conscription has helped to

defuse aggression, imposing a highly structured environment upon dangerous individuals at the peak of their criminal energies. Crime rates typically plummet during wartime and immediately following the cessation of war. In some cases, however, military training has merely provided an extended tutorial in the techniques of killing that has fed criminal careers (e.g., Timothy McVeigh).

Another reason we shouldn't be surprised by violent children is that American history and folklore are rich with examples of bad kids blazing their way across the plains. Jesse James was seventeen years old when he rode with Quantrill's Confederate guerrillas—a gang of murderous psychopaths that justified its viciousness with paramilitary rhetoric. By the age of nineteen, James had committed his first murder. William H. Bonney—Billy the Kid—was even more precocious, slaying his first victim at the tender age of fourteen. By his twenty-first birthday, he'd left twenty-one dead men behind. Butch Cassidy began rustling cattle during early adolescence and graduated to robbing trains before he was twenty. Clyde Barrow, of Bonnie and Clyde notoriety, was judged an incorrigible truant, thief, and runaway at *nine* and committed his first armed robbery only a few years later. Murder followed soon after.

One of our most frightening and unrepentant criminals, labeled "the complete misanthrope" by crime historian Robert Jay Nash, was a charming fellow born a century ago named Carl Panzram, who evinced criminal tendencies almost from the crib (65).

"Dedicated to the wholesale destruction of mankind," as Nash terms him, Panzram began his criminal career with an arrest for drunk and disorderly behavior at the age of *eight*, went on a robbery rampage at eleven, set fire to a warehouse at seventeen, robbed, assaulted, and burned throughout his adolescence, and capped his accomplishments with the robbery, sodomy, and murder of at least ten men. (Panzram claimed twenty-one victims, including children.) Jack Henry Abbott, Norman Mailer's protégé, dedicated *In the Belly of the Beast* to Panzram. Perhaps Mailer and others should have taken the hint.

Not that admiration of psychopaths is limited to other psychopaths. The fact that American folklore has lionized the likes of Billy the Kid, Jesse James, and Bonnie and Clyde, elevating them to folk heroes, combined with our general glorification of the brutal and violent periods such as the Wild West, may tell us something about our true feelings toward youthful murderousness.

We decry the latest schoolyard rampage, but soon we're back to singing adulatory ballads about bad kids and flocking to movies about young guns. Talk about mixed messages.

That same confused attitude was exhibited, to terrible effect, within the family of Kipland Kinkel, the fifteen-year-old who murdered his parents and shot up a school in Springfield, Oregon, killing two students and wounding twenty-two others.

For years, Kinkel's parents had complained to friends and neighbors about their fear of their son. And with good reason. Kip had long displayed classical characteristics of violent psychopathy: cruelty to animals, sadism, a previous arrest for throwing rocks at cars from an overpass, attention deficit combined with learning problems, multiple school suspensions, and an obsession with weapons and explosives. Efforts to remedy the situation included Ritalin, Prozac, short-term psychiatric counseling, and overindulgence— summer trips to Spain and Costa Rica, lessons in tennis, sailing, and skiing. An attempt to sublimate Kip's aggression with martial arts training resulted in a school suspension for karate-kicking another boy in the head. Soon after, Kip threw a pencil at another boy and was suspended yet again (66).

Kip was reinforced for his behavior by being allowed to remain out of school. Mr. and Mrs. Kinkel, both teachers, took turns instructing their son at home. Friends describe them as dedicated, hardworking parents whose other child, an older sister, was a model student.

Yet Kip remained impervious to their efforts, boasting about stuffing firecrackers into a cat's mouth and reading aloud in class from a journal in which he wrote about plans to "kill everybody." He learned about explosives on the Internet, built five bombs, and hid them in crawl spaces around the family home.

This was the boy Mr. and Mrs. Kinkel chose to favor with a semiautomatic Ruger rifle and two handguns. The rifle was the weapon Kip used to kill them and to fire fifty rounds into the cafeteria at Thurston High.

One hesitates to blame victims. But . . . *why on earth?*

When I practiced psychology it wasn't at all rare to encounter parents who brought a child for treatment and expressed great distress about the identified problem, but turned ambivalent and resistant when the patient began to improve.

Sometimes ambivalence showed itself right from the beginning, like the father who bemoaned his son's bullying tendencies during an intake session, only to smile at me across the desk and add, "He *is* pretty tough. Doesn't take guff from anyone." Other displays were more subtle—a wink and a nod, failure to comply with a treatment plan, failure to bring the child back once a treatment plan had been devised. I encountered parents who grew openly resentful toward the child *after* he got better and tried actively to undermine the therapeutic process. One particularly hostile mother went so far as to overdose on her seriously depressed daughter's antidepressants.

From what I could tell, this shift typically occurred when the child had been labeled the primary or sole problem in a *systemically* malfunctioning family. Focusing exclusively upon a problem child is easy to do even in cohesive families, because difficult kids do demand and receive a tremendous amount of attention. But there can also be defensive value in scapegoating and concentrating solely on the identified patient, as it allows everyone else to ignore their own problems.

Could that have been part of what was going on when Bill and Faith Kinkel rewarded their flagrantly dangerous son with an instant collection of lethal weapons? Was there some need to keep Kip *bad*? Or had these poor parents simply been beaten down by years of threats and rage and finally relented out of fear of what Kip might do if they continued to frustrate his lust for guns?

Whatever the reason, giving in was a tragic error that signed their death warrants and those of two children.

The backgrounds of Andrew Golden and Mitchell Johnson, though not as conspicuously psychopathic as Kinkel's, are also in accordance with what we know about dangerous kids. Initial accounts of the Arkansas pair described two normal-sounding country boys—Tom Sawyer and Huck Finn with speed loaders. But as information filtered in, quite another picture materialized.

Andrew's grandmother described him as an all-American kid, but neighbors labeled him as mean-spirited and recalled his strutting around the neighborhood with a hunting knife strapped to his leg (67).

"We knew the kid was evil," said one local, "but never that evil."

Like many juvenile slayers, Golden grew up in a household obsessed with firearms. His father was an officer of the Practical Pistol Shooters club, and he introduced Andrew to lethal weapons at a very young age, snapping photos of the boy at six, staring, rather cold-eyed, down the barrel of a pistol. Andrew's grandfather, from whom most of the Jonesboro massacre weapons were stolen, bragged about Andrew's killing his first duck the previous year—bragged *after* the schoolyard shootings. Even allowing for rural norms that encourage hunting and shooting as male-bonding experiences, all this seems more than a bit worshipful of bloodletting.

Mitchell Johnson, claimed by his mother to be just a regular kid from a regular family, was anything but. A police chief in the Minnesota town of Grand Meadow, where Mitchell spent his early childhood, described the boy as highly troubled, with a chronic tendency to wander away from home that suggests early neglect.

During a visit to the Johnson house, this same officer noticed a .357 pistol sitting on the kitchen table, in full view and reach of eight-year-old Mitchell, and warned the parents about it. The officer forbade his own children to associate with Mitchell.

Paternal risk factors also loom large in Mitchell's history. His father was fired for theft. His mother, a prison guard, obtained a divorce and moved with Mitchell to Jonesboro in order to join her new boyfriend, an ex-con incarcerated for drug and firearms crimes at the very prison where she'd worked. Shortly after, she married this felon and he became Mitchell's stepfather.

Mitchell had long attracted attention as a troubled kid. He bragged that he smoked heroin and had joined a gang, warned he might commit suicide, and finally, broadcast his intentions by exclaiming, "I've got a lot of killing to do."

Neglectful parenting, broken home, criminal father, criminal stepfather, a mother whose choices—selection of two criminals as spouses, leaving a loaded pistol in front of a grade-schooler—suggest less than optimal judgment, guns, guns, guns. Sound familiar?

These are the kids we teach to speed-load and to shoot semiautomatic weapons?

Which leads us to the single most important step we can take, in the short run, to preventing child criminality: Restrict access to firearms.

No matter how much time is spent drilling young psychopaths in the art and etiquette of "practical shooting," they will inevitably use firearms to victimize others, precisely the way Kip Kinkel utilized his karate skills. Given the ease with which we allow kids and guns to interact, we have no right to be astonished at incidents of headline-grabbing carnage accomplished by dangerous boys. Once again, the chief surprise is that it doesn't happen more often.

Back off, NRA, I'm not talking about trampling on any adult's constitutional right to bear arms. Let's sidestep the entire gun-control debate but accept the painfully obvious fact that no *kids* should ever be allowed access to pistols, rifles, and shotguns. Children and teens are simply insufficiently socialized to handle implements designed, no matter how you gussy them up with clubs and guilds and marksmanship contests, to *kill*. We restrict minors from driving and establish a minimum age for voting because we understand the principle that minors have not yet attained full reasoning capability. Why in the world do we continue to allow them to play around with Rugers and Colts and Mosslers?

The very fact that we even *debate* the point seems ludicrous. Then again, we are the country that lionizes the likes of Billy the Kid.

When I proposed restricting children's access to lethal weapons in my *USA Today* column, I received irate mail from gun freaks letting me know I'd missed the point completely and was probably a mushy-minded social reformer. The culprit for schoolyard shootings and similar abominations, according to these geniuses, wasn't access to weapons, it was some nebulous concept labeled "societal breakdown."

Fine. Let's assume society has indeed deteriorated

to the point of damaging the psychological stability of our youngsters. Isn't that all the *more* reason to keep them away from Messrs. Smith and Wesson et alia? The reluctance to make these commonsense decisions is truly astonishing.

If separating kids from guns violates some rural or good-ol'-boy norm, so be it. It's a *bad* norm. Wanna bond with your son? Go hiking, toss the football, play catch. Or even—and *this* is radical—sit down and *talk* to him. Maybe you can even discuss what masculinity is all about, how to temper assertiveness with kindness, why avoiding violence can be braver and more effective than lashing out.

Yes, I'm talking about that old sissy stuff. The kind of effete chatter that leads to introspection rather than mass destruction. The kind of softhearted, softheaded mollycoddling that may even protect some little girl or boy from being sighted like quail on the hot asphalt of a schoolyard.

Sure, a black market will develop in response to such gun laws, as it does with any prohibition. And sure, urban gangbangers will continue to get hold of weaponry. But the likes of Golden, Johnson, and Kinkel are a lot more likely to be inhibited from taking up arms in the service of psychopathy. They got *their* arsenals from Mom and Dad and Gramps.

Restricting children from having access to firearms should be backed up with real judicial muscle—quick and unconditional imposition of jail or reformatory sentences for possession of pistols, rifles, or shotguns for youthful offenders, and even longer jail time, combined with outrageously high monetary fines, for the adults who allow guns to fall into the hands of minors. Zero tolerance is needed because the stakes are high. It's worked to almost completely eliminate drunk driving in the Scandinavian countries, in the absence of any concomitant decrease in overall Scandinavian alcoholism.

Two other quick fixes: The first is to *take the warnings of violent kids seriously*. When they say they're going to kill someone, they mean it. Arrest them for making terrorist threats. The second is to *take your time figuring out what to do with them*. Be extremely reluctant to release them back into the community. (I'm no constitutional scholar, but the fact that we routinely restrict the rights of minors via curfew laws and limited licenses suggests there would be few successful legal challenges to this type of preventative custody.) And second, when youngsters murder coldly, lock them up till they die.

Now for long-term solutions.

If, as the evidence suggests, a cold emotional system is most frequently the result of maltreatment, we need to focus our attention much more consistently and assiduously upon the detection, prevention, and remediation of child neglect and abuse. Policies that emphasize reintegration of the abused child into his family need to be looked at extremely critically. Obviously, if biological parents are motivated to change, we need to work with them. However, by insisting on "family unification" at all costs, in many cases we are simply tossing bait to the sharks. Loving, warm, caring foster care and adoptive homes are optimal solutions, but bad foster homes are worse than good, or even mediocre, institutional care.

Though the notion of large-scale orphanages and similar group placements may evoke Dickensian images, well-designed group settings are significantly kinder and more helpful places and better vehicles for moral training for abused children than are bad homes (68). Some of the most productive and ethical citizens around are members of my parents' generation, individuals orphaned during the world wars and raised in quality orphanages.

Along with vigilantly locating abused and neglected kids, we need to embark on an extremely aggressive search for, and identification of, youngsters at risk for violent criminality. There will be substantial overlap between the two processes.

With regard to picking out the dangerous kids, there is no need to fund commissions or to dissect the problem academically. We already *know* whom to look for: those who display precocious aggression and antisocial behavior, reactive or proactive, for whatever reason. A relatively tiny but important sample.

In some cases the families that spawn youngsters who lean toward criminality may be workable, and all attempts should be made to retrain bad parents as well as dangerous kids—but not at the expense of the children.

In other instances a draconian solution will be necessary: abrogation of parental custody and removal of children from the violent, chaotic homes most likely to raise habitual criminals. This needs to occur *well before adolescence*. As noted, data about age as it relates to rehabilitation are absent. My clinical hunch is that by the time a seriously violent boy is eleven or twelve, in most cases it may be too late to modify his behavior meaningfully. And in fact, research has shown that police contact before eleven is an extremely strong predictor of a lifetime of criminality (69). This may be because of neurological changes that commonly occur in the frontal and prefrontal lobes around this period, "hard-wiring" patterns of behavior (70).

Assuming we locate high-risk youngsters, what next? Conventional, insight-oriented psychotherapy is of little use when dealing with antisocial behavior. Techniques do exist, however, that *can* help.

High-risk kids need to be placed in very structured, loving environments, free of abuse, where punishment is noncorporal and is used at a minuscule level. Nonviolent behavior needs to be taught to them as if they are majoring in morality, using explicit lessons delivered by warm, caring adult disciplinarians who control the rewards their young charges receive. Goodies must be contingent upon attainment of prosocial behavioral goals mapped out in detail, such as courtesy, empathy, kindness, and nonviolent problem solving, as well as academic achievement.

Yes, we're talking about behavior therapy. Notwithstanding the sad case of Alex, the recidivist fictional thug-hero of *A Clockwork Orange*, behavior therapy works extremely well when properly and consistently directed at children young enough to still be emotionally and ethically malleable, and when combined with backup treatments that address biological deficiencies. (Burgess's novel featured a specific type of aversive Pavlovian conditioning, punishment for bad thoughts—a technique that would not be expected to work very well with psychopaths. And Alex was already far too old for any kind of "treatment.")

High-risk kids need to receive intensive *schooling in morality*—consistent, structured, detailed lessons about ethics, honesty, and consideration for others, as well as finely tuned behavioral tutoring in specific methods of dealing with moral issues and puzzles. Children leaning toward criminality who also suffer from learning disabilities and hyperactivity—a substantial majority— will also require extensive academic coaching for the former and medication for the latter.

Though I have dismissed psychotherapy as a primary treatment for psychopathy—an assertion no serious student of the subject would dispute—this does not imply that we should never talk to these kids about their problems nor allow them to express their feelings (appropriately). We must never forget that most of them have been conceived in chaos and raised with cruelty. Morality training will not work unless it is carried out in an atmosphere of genuine warmth and affection—first, because all kids need to be listened to and to be valued, and second, because one of the most effective ways of teaching is by example. If we want to turn high-risk kids into empathetic, caring human beings, they must be on the receiving end of empathy and caring.

So counseling for behavioral manifestations of sadness and fear and loneliness *does* have a role in moral training. But in the case of violent kids, the first priority needs to be changing maladaptive patterns of behavior. Precocious violence sets up self-fulfilling prophecies of its own and is so obstructive and damaging in the way it blocks out appropriate emotions and positive behaviors that counseling is likely to be ineffective until the violence is eliminated.

We need to get high-risk kids to a point where they can *do good things*. Only then can they earn rewards for being moral and generate a positive learning cycle that overpowers the learned-violence paradigm of their former lives.

This comprehensive approach remains, sadly, an ideal. Removal of high-risk kids from rotten homes assumes that there's somewhere to put them, and we are far from that situation. It is also predicated upon the availability of an army of experts to teach criminally inclined boys the explicit dimensions of moral behavior and nonviolent, nonexploitative methods of obtaining stimulation, as well as platoons of tutors and physicians working to remediate learning disabilities.

But the talent and techniques do exist. What we need is the will and the courage to suggest and implement strong solutions. Would it be expensive? Not at all, given the savings, human and financial, that accrue when crime rates plummet and the energies of high-risk youngsters are redirected toward industry and away from interaction with the welfare and the criminal justice systems. Currently we are experiencing sharp drops in crime across the country. Some of the decrease can be attributed to more industrious policing and longer prison sentences of the "three strikes" variety. But a good chunk is also due to a factor we *cannot* control: demographics, namely, the fact that there are fewer males in the fifteen- to twenty-year-old age range. Population profiles change cyclically, so let's not get too complacent. Eventually there will come a time when the proportion of violent youth rises sharply, and no policing or imprisoning will completely handle the tide of crimes they will commit. Wouldn't it be smart to be prepared?

Where will the money for group placement and moral training come from? Certainly no new taxes should be levied. That would be impolitic as well as unnecessary. Nor should funds be leeched by the

Washington reflex to create commissions and commit-
tees. We don't *have* to discuss the issue ad nauseam. We
already know what needs to be done.

For progress to be made, the romanticization of
childhood to the point where it leads to head-in-the-
sand denial about the brutal realities of abused children
and the harsh realities of psychopathy needs to cease.

Boys will be boys, but violent boys will be
dangerous.

Money should be transferred from dead-end research
areas, such as media violence, into clinical programs for
early identification and treatment of pathological childhood aggression.

We need to stop paying for programs that are
doomed to failure, such as a project I recently read
about where high-school students were to be offered a
three-week cable TV series that preached against the
use of violence. First of all, by the time kids are in
high school it's too late. Second, three weeks of video
indoctrination is unlikely to accomplish anything.
Third, the measure of success used—filling out a
questionnaire about aggression—has no relevance to
real-life violence. And finally, targeting entire school
bodies is preaching to the converted.

Forget about global approaches that attempt to
change entire ethnic groups or neighborhoods. They're
as sensible as giving chemotherapy to patients without
cancer. It's a lot smarter—and cheaper—to focus upon
a very small but dangerous minority: the really scary kids.

Even if there exists a small subsample of well-brought-up children for whom cold-bloodedness and subsequent psychopathy are totally inborn genetic traits, there is no reason to throw up our hands. Genetically linked behaviors, though they may be resistant to change, *can* be modified by the environment. Take the case of phenylketonuria (PKU), a metabolic disorder that once led inevitably to severe mental retardation. Now it is completely treatable with dietary manipulation. Two other triumphs of environmental tinkering with genetically mediated defects are so commonplace that we no longer give them a second thought: eyeglasses and orthodonture.

This is not to say that fixing genetic psychopathy is as simple as straightening an overbite or clearing up a myopic haze. But changing the environment *can* alter genetic variables.

I have worked personally with numerous children, such as retarded youngsters and those with genetic defects, whose severe behavioral problems were related to inborn factors but who responded extremely well to behavior therapy. One particularly fascinating case that I published in 1977 was the treatment of a seven-year-old boy with a condition known as 47XYY karyotype—possession of an extra male chromosome.

First discovered in 1961, 47XYY was implicated in violent, aggressive, antisocial behavior when the trait was found to exist in a disproportionately high number of Scottish prison inmates. Several years later, an extremely notorious XYY surfaced—mass murderer Richard Speck—and criminal defense attorneys rushed to create a genetic apologia for violence. For a while the strategy worked, as some defendants were actually acquitted because of chromosomal abnormalities and others had their sentences reduced (71). Subsequent research showed the original Scottish tabulations to be flawed—based upon an incorrect frequency of 47XYY in the noncriminal population—and several other studies revealed no link between the extra male chromosome and criminality.

Whatever the cause for the behavioral problems of the boy I saw—let's call him Bobby—he was more than a handful and needed to be dealt with immediately.

I treated Bobby in the same room where I'd attempted to connect with Tim. Barely seven, he was small, skinny, blond, and blue-eyed, was mildly retarded (IQ score of 79), displayed symptoms of hyperactivity despite treatment with Ritalin, and had unclear speech. Three mild but noticeable physical abnormalities were present: an extremely weak chin, shortened index fingers, and a small skull. Bobby's parents were happily married, and he was their only child. At the time of his birth, Bobby's mother was thirty-nine. His delivery had been normal. However, she had suffered three previous miscarriages.

Bobby's problem behaviors included defiance, refusal to feed himself and storing food in his cheeks, insomnia and interrupting his parents' sleep, aggression against playmates, public masturbation, hitting and biting his parents, and tantrums so severe they included the hurling of furniture and other large objects. He'd shattered all the windows in the family home, and the panes had been replaced by panels of plastic. His pediatrician had prescribed the Ritalin for his hyperactivity, and though the drug had been partially effective, it had produced no carryover to other areas.

Bobby's physical problems were conspicuous, so the temptation to attribute his behavioral problems to organic, unmodifiable causes was strong, even though it was by no means clear that any of his difficulties were related to the extra chromosome (most XYYs are of normal intelligence).

From the parents' account during history taking, this kid sounded like a little monster. Yet when I met him, Bobby was pleasant, cooperative, and extremely responsive to praise. Furthermore, his behavior at the special school he attended was not reported to be troublesome. This led me to suspect that the ways his parents dealt with his behavior—notably, giving him attention when he was disruptive—might be a factor.

Fortunately, Bobby's parents were highly motivated and devoid of the ambivalence I've discussed previously. Their son's behavior had driven them—almost literally—to their wits' end.

I developed rapport with Bobby quite easily using play therapy and was able to work with the entire family. The details of the treatment plan can be found in a previously published technical article, but the general approach was nothing revolutionary: helping the parents develop behavior goals and then showing them how to reward good behavior while ignoring and/or punishing bad behavior (72). They were quite successful at following through, and within weeks Bobby's behavior had improved dramatically. Tantrums had decreased to a third of the previous rate, the destructive behavior had disappeared, and Bobby was sleeping through the night and feeding himself, though he continued to be a picky eater (probably related to appetite loss from the Ritalin). Furthermore, some behaviors we hadn't yet targeted had also improved: Bobby was talking more, initiating conversations, and speaking in longer sentences. His speech was also clearer, and his father was amazed that he could now carry on a conversation with his son. This probably occurred because high-rate disruption can be thought of as "behavioral garbage," hogging so much time that it often suppresses speech (73).

Within weeks, Bobby's parents were able to eliminate the evening dose of Ritalin and to go away on vacation by themselves, leaving Bobby with a baby-sitter. She reported the boy had been just fine.

The one behavior that didn't change early on was inappropriate masturbation. I showed the parents how to use a mild punishment technique called time-out (having Bobby sit in a corner for several minutes) each time he masturbated publicly. Within a month, this problem was reduced to 25 percent of its former frequency.

A follow-up four months later showed stability in Bobby's gains. Bobby was now sleeping so soundly that his mother sometimes had to wake him up in the morning.

I am no miracle worker. The psychological literature is full of thousands of success stories accomplished by the systematic, humane application of behavioral principles to problem behaviors. I believe that if we catch antisocial kids early enough, they too will be amenable to behavioral treatment. We need to approach psychopathy with rational optimism and intellectual strength, confident in the knowledge that no society is more capable than ours and that we are doing the right thing.

Andrew Golden, Mitchell Johnson, Kipland Kinkel, and others like them have wrought suffering beyond description. But if widespread revulsion at the horrors perpetrated by these young criminals leads us to correct choices, perhaps they have taught us valuable lessons without intending to.

If we remain clearheaded, do what needs to be done, and are successful in preventing other tragedies, a bit of solace may yet be drawn from Jonesboro, Springfield, and so many other American killing fields.

Bibliography

1. Rachuba, L., et al. Violent crime in the United States: An epidemiologic profile. *Arch. Pediatrics & Adolescent Medicine,* September 1995, 953–60.
2. Loeber, R. Antisocial behavior: More enduring than changeable. *J. Amer. Acad. Child & Adol. Psychiatry,* May 1991, 393–97.
3. Frick, P. J., et al. Psychopathy and conduct problems in children. *J. Abn. Psychol.,* November 1994, 700–7.
4. Mitchell, S., and Rosa, P. Boyhood behavior problems as precursors of criminality: A fifteen-year follow-up study. *J. Child. Psychol. Psychiat.,* November 1979, 19–33.
5. Brook, J. S., et al. Young adult drug use and delinquency: Childhood antecedents and adolescent mediators. *J. Amer. Acad. Child & Adoles. Psychiat.,* December 1996, 1584–92.
6. Brook, J. S., and Newcomb, M.D. Childhood aggression and unconventionality: Impact on later academic achievement, drug use, and workforce involvement. *J. Genet. Psychol.,* December 1995, 393–410.

7. Hart, S. D., et al. Performance of male psychopaths following conditional release from prison. *J. Consult. Clin. Psychol.,* April 1988, 227–32.

8. Dodge, K. A., et al. Reactive and proactive aggression in schoolchildren and psychiatrically impaired chronically assaultive youth. *J. Abn. Psychol.,* February 1997, 37–51.

9. Zagar, R., et al. Homicidal adolescents: A replication. *Psychol. Reports,* December 1990, 1235–42.

10. Myers, W. C., et al. Psychopathology, biopsychosocial factors, crime characteristics and classification of 25 homicidal youths. *J. Amer. Acad. Child & Adol. Psychiat.,* November 1995, 1483–89.

11. Cornell, D. G., et al. Juvenile homicide: Prior adjustment and a proposed typology. *Amer. J. Orthopsychiat.,* July 1987, 383–93.

12. Lewis, D. O., et al. Biopsychosocial characteristics of children who later murder: A prospective study. *Amer. J. Psychiat.,* October 1985, 1161–67.

13. Myers, W. C., et al. Criminal and behavioral aspects of juvenile sexual homicide. *J. Forensic Sci.,* 1989, 340–47.

14. Ascione, F. R. Children who are cruel to animals: A review of research implications for developmental psychopathology. *Anthrozoos,* 1993, 226–47.

15. Monroe, L. J., and Marks, P. A. Psychotherapists' descriptions of emotionally disturbed adolescent poor and good sleepers. *J. Clin. Psychol.,* January 1977, 263–69.

16. Kellerman, J. Pearls, yet swine. *Modern Painters,* Spring 1996, 56–59.

17. Millar, T. P. The age of passion man. *Canad J. Psychiat.,* December 1982, 679–82.

18. Mailer, N. The white negro. *Dissent,* 1957.

19. Hazelwood, R. Serial rapists. *FBI Law Enforcement Bulletin,* January 1989, 11–25.

20. Lewis, C. E. Neurochemical mechanisms of chronic anti-social behavior (psychopathy): A literature review. *J. Nerv. Ment. Disease,* December 1991, 720–27.

21. Patrick, C. J., et al. Emotion in the criminal psychopath: Fear image processing. *J. Abn. Psychol.,* August 1994, 523–34.

22. Lidberg, L., et al. Urinary catecholamines, stress and psychopathy: A study of arrested men awaiting trial. *Psychosom. Medicine,* March 1978, 116–25.

23. Reuters wire release, March 25, 1998.

24. Hodgins, S., et al. Mental disorder and crime. *Arch. Gen. Psychiat.,* January 1998, 86–88.

25. Lewis, D. O., et al. Neuropsychiatric, psychoeducational, and family characteristics of 14 juveniles condemned to death in the United States. *Amer. J. Psychiat.,* May 1988, 584–89.

26. Jamison, K. R. *An unquiet mind.* NY: Knopf, 1995.

27. Harper, T. J., et al. Factor structure of the Psychopathy Checklist. *J. Consult. Clin. Psychol.,* October 1988, 741–47.

28. Deuteronomy 21:18–21.

29. Babylonian Talmud, Tractate Sanhedrin, chapter eight: *Ben Sorer Umoreh.*

30. Blackburn, R., and Lee-Evans, J. M. Reactions of primary and secondary psychopaths to anger-evoking situations. *Brit. J. Clin. Psychol.,* May 1985, 93–100.

31. Rydelius, P. A. Alcohol-abusing teenage boys: Testing a hypothesis on the relationship between alcohol abuse and social background factors, criminality and personality in teenage boys. *Acta Psychiatrica Scandinavica,* November 1983, 368–80.

32. Moss, H. B., et al. Aggressivity among sons of substance-abusing fathers: Association with psychiatric disorder in the father and son, paternal personality, pubertal development, and socioeconomic status. *Am. J. Drug & Alcohol Abuse,* May 1995, 195–208.

33. Myers, M. G., et al. Progression from conduct disorder to

antisocial personality disorder following treatment for adolescent substance abuse. *Am. J. Psychiat.*, April 1998, 479–85.

34. Dabbs, J. M., et al. Age, testosterone, and behavior among female prison inmates. *Psychosom. Med.*, September/October 1997, 477–80.

35. Hare, R. D., et al. Male psychopaths and their criminal careers. *J. Consult. Clin. Psychol.*, October 1988, 710–14.

36. Campbell, C., et al. Prevalence and impact of exposure to interpersonal violence among suburban and urban middle school students. *Pediatrics*, September 1996, 396–402.

37. Straus, M. A. Spanking and the making of a violent society. *Pediatrics*, October 1996, 837–42.

38. McCord, J. Questioning the value of punishment. *Soc. Prob.*, 1991, 167–79.

39. Aber, J. L. Poverty, violence, and child development: Untangling family and community level effects. In Charles A. Nelson (ed.), *Threats to optimal development: Integrating biological, psychological, and social risk factors.* The Minnesota Symposia, vol. 27. Hillsdale, NJ: Lawrence Erlbaum Associates, 1994, 229–72.

40. Samenow, S. E. *Inside the criminal mind.* NY: Times Books, 1984.

41. Kosson, D. S., et al. Evaluating the construct validity of psychopathy in black and white male inmates: Three preliminary studies. *J. Abn. Psychol.*, August 1990, 250–59.

42. Dennis, P. M. Chills and thrills: Does radio harm our children? The controversy over program violence during the age of radio. *J. Hist. Behav. Sci.*, Winter 1998, 33–50.

43. Heath, L., et al. Effects of media violence on children: A review of the literature. *Arch. Gen. Psychiat.*, June 1990, 595–96.

44. Bushman, B. J. Moderating role of trait aggressiveness in the effects of violent media on aggression. *J. Person. Soc. Psychol.*, November 1995, 950–60.

45. Black, D., and Newman, M. Television violence and children. *Brit. Med. J.,* February 1995, 273–74.

46. Heilbrun, A. B., and Heilbrun, M. R. Psychopathy and dangerousness: Comparison, integration and extension of two psychopathic typologies. *Brit. J. Clin. Psychol.,* September 1985, 181–95.

47. Hart, S. D., et al. Performance of criminal psychopaths on selected neuropsychological tests. *J. Abn. Psychol.,* November 1990, 374–79.

48. Patrick, C. J., et al. Emotion in the criminal psychopath: Startle reflex modulation. *J. Abn. Psychol.,* February 1993, 82–92.

49. Williamson, S., et al. Abnormal processing of affective words by psychopaths. *Psychophysiology,* May 1991, 260–73.

50. Raine, A. Antisocial behavior and psychophysiology: A biosocial perspective and a prefrontal dysfunction hypothesis. In D. M. Stoff et al. (eds.), *Handbook of Antisocial Behavior.* NY: John Wiley & Sons, 1997, 289–303.

51. Raine, A., et al. Brain abnormalities in murderers indicated by positron emission tomography. *Biol. Psychiat.,* 1997, 495–508.

52. Halperin, J., et al. Serotonin, aggression and parental psychopathology in children with attention-deficit hyperactivity disorder. *Am. Acad. Child & Adol. Psychiat.,* October 1997, 1391–98.

53. Kindlon, D., et al. Longitudinal patterns of heart rate and fighting behavior in 9 through 12 year old boys. *Am. Acad. Child & Adol. Psychiat.,* March 1995, 371–77.

54. Raine, A., et al. Low resting heart rate at age 3 years predisposes to aggression at age 11 years: Evidence from the Mauritius Child Health Project. *J. Am. Acad. Child & Adol. Psychiat.,* October 1997, 1457–64.

55. Raine, A., et al. High autonomic arousal and electrodermal orienting at age 15 as protective factors against criminal

behavior at age 29 years. *Am J. Psychiat.*, November 1995, 1595–1600.

56. Raine, A., et al. Relationships between central and autonomic measures of arousal at age 15 years and criminality at age 24 years. *Arch. Gen. Psychiat.*, November 1990, 1003–7.

57. Brennan, P., et al. Psychophysiological protective factors for male subjects at high risk for criminal behavior. *Am J. Psychiat.*, June 1997, 853–55.

58. Raine, A., et al. Interaction between birth complications and early maternal rejection in predisposing individuals to adult violence: Specificity to serious, early-onset violence. *Am. J. Psychiat.*, September 1997, 1265–71.

59. Raine, A., et al. High rates of violence, crime, academic problems and behavioral problems in males with both early neuromotor deficits and unstable family environments. *Arch. Gen. Psychiat.*, June 1996, 544–49.

60. Wadsworth, M. E. Delinquency, pulse rate and early emotional deprivation. *Brit. J. Psychiat.*, 1987, 668–73.

61. Cenci, M. A., et al. Regional differences in the regulation of dopamine and noradrenaline release in medial frontal cortex, nucleus accumbens and caudate-putamen: A microdialysis study in the rat. *Brain Research,* 1992, 217–28.

62. Walsh, A., et al. Violent delinquents: An examination of psychopathic typologies. *J. Genet. Psychol.*, September 1987, 385–92.

63. Forth, A. E., and Hare, R. D. The contingent negative variation in psychopaths. *Psychophysiology,* November 1989, 676–82.

64. Kahsani, J. H., et al. Intrafamilial homicide committed by juveniles: Examination of a sample with recommendations for prevention. *J. Forensic Sci.*, 1997, 873–78.

65. Nash, J. R. *Bloodletters and Badmen.* NY: Warner Books, 1982.

66. Kasindorf, M. Parents struggled to control their son. *USA Today,* May 26, 1997, 3A.

67. Gegax, T. T., et al. The boys behind the ambush. *Newsweek,* April 6, 1998.

68. Timm, J. T. Group care of children and development of moral judgment. *Child Welfare,* June 1980, 323–33.

69. Christian, R. E., et al. Psychopathy and conduct problems in children: II. Implications for subtyping children with conduct problems. *J. Am. Acad. Child & Adol. Psychiat.,* February 1997, 233–41.

70. Matthews, L. Personal communication, August 1998.

71. Kessler, S., and Moos, R. H. The XYY karyotype and criminality: A review. *J. Psychiatr. Research,* 1970, 153–70.

72. Kellerman, J. Behavioral treatment of a boy with 47XYY karyotype. *J. Nerv. Ment. Disease,* 1977, 67–71.

73. Risley, R., and Wolf, M. Establishing functional speech in echolalic children. *Behav. Res. Ther.,* 1967, 73–88.

Index

ABOUT THE AUTHOR

The recipient of numerous awards for achievement in fiction writing and psychology, JONATHAN KELLERMAN is the author of three volumes on psychology, two books for children, and two dozen bestselling crime novels, as well as scores of research studies and essays published in scientific and popular journals. He has won the Goldwyn, Edgar, and Anthony awards, and has been nominated for a Shamus Award.

Trained as a child clinical psychologist, Dr. Kellerman was founding director of the Psychosocial Program, Children's Hospital of Los Angeles, and was clinical professor of pediatrics at the University of Southern California School of Medicine and clinical professor of psychology at USC's College of Arts and Sciences. He and his wife, bestselling novelist Faye Kellerman live in California and New Mexico. Their four children include the novelist Jesse Kellerman. Visit the author's website at www.jonathankellerman.com.

A Note on The Library of Contemporary Thought

This exciting new series tackles today's most provocative, fascinating, and relevant issues, giving top opinion makers a forum to explore topics that matter urgently to themselves and their readers. Some will be think pieces. Some will be research oriented. Some will be journalistic in nature. The form is wide open, but the aim is the same: to say things that need saying.

Also available from
**THE LIBRARY OF CONTEMPORARY
THOUGHT**

*America's most original writers
give you a piece of their minds*

Robert Hughes
Walter Mosley
Joe Klein
Don Imus
Donna Tartt
Nora Ephron